Learning Journey
on the
Red Road

Learning Journey on the
Red Road

Floyd Looks for Buffalo Hand

**Edited by
Marc Alexander Huminilowycz**

Learning Journey On The Red Road. Copyright © 1998 by Floyd Looks for Buffalo Hand. All Rights reserved. No part of this book may be reproduced or utilized in any form or by any electronic or mechanical means, including information storage and retrieval devices or systems, without prior written permission from the author - except in the case of brief quotations embodied in critical articles and reviews.

Edited by Marc Alexander Huminilowycz
Cover Inspiration: Philip Coté
Book Design: Andy Ip
Production: Warren Fisher
Portrait Photography: Kirk McGregor
Still Photography: David So

Printed and bound in Canada

Canadian Cataloguing in Publication Data

Hand, Floyd Looks for Buffalo, 1939-
      Learning journey on the red road

Includes index.
ISBN   0-9663957-0-0

1. Hand, Floyd Looks for Buffalo, 1939- . I. Huminilowycz, Marc Alexander II. Title.

E99.03H362 1998   299'.7852   C98-931035-3

To order copies of **Learning Journey on the Red Road**, please indicate quantity required and send check or money order for $14.95 U.S./$19.95 Canadian plus shipping & handling ($4.00 for first book, $1.00 for each additional book) to: Learning Journey Communications, 24 Orchard Crescent, Toronto, Ontario M8Z 3E1. Canadian residents please add 7% GST to total order. Please allow 4-6 weeks for delivery. For phone/fax orders, requests for review copies or bookseller/library/educational institution inquiries, **call/fax (416)231-3118** in Toronto area or toll-free **1-800-713-7395**. E-mail address: journey@better.net

The author is available for teaching circles, speaking engagements and interviews. Please contact: Floyd Looks for Buffalo Hand, P.O. Box 150, Pine Ridge, South Dakota 57770. Tel: (605)867-5762 Fax: (605)867-2115

Contents

Pilamaya - Thank You

I dedicate Learning Journey on the Red Road to the greatest teacher of all, Frank Young Man Afraid of His Horses, who gave me a vision and a dream, and to all the beautiful women and men who came to teach me after him - especially Emma White Cow Killer, Susanna Hand Red Cloud, Martin High Bear, James Dubray and Amos Owen.

This book would not have been possible without the help of both my immediate family and my "Hunka" extended families - mothers Zona, Doreen and Sadie, Eagle Pipe Woman, Kills Crow Woman, Star Buffalo, Itunkala Ohitika, Win Ole, Egle and Marc Huminilowycz, and Lora and Richard Dart.

I thank the Oglala Nation (the Grass Roots People) for their support. And I thank my elders and all my relatives throughout the nations, who encouraged me to pass on these teachings and educate the younger generations and relatives throughout this world. These days, I am not able to travel and talk to people as much as I would like to. So I wish to pass on to the people this dedication to the Red Road, in respect of my ancestors. This is my personal learning that I must share.

To my mom and dad, Marie and Floyd, my greatest gratitude for bringing me into this world to serve the people. And I send my love to my brothers and sisters - Irby, Alton, Arlene and Donna.

Author's Note

These days, if you go to a book store or your local library, you will find dozens of books about Indian culture, history and spirituality. But most of them have been written by authors of European ancestry - from a left-brained European perspective. *Learning Journey on the Red Road* is a different book. It is based upon my own teachings and my Indian way of life. It is about the way traditional Indian people live - according to the circle of life, the psychology of life. The teachings and messages contained in these pages come from the right brain. They come from the heart.

Understand that this is not a storybook, with a beginning and an ending. Just as the Sacred White Buffalo teachings are seven separate journeys, *Learning Journey on the Red Road* is a collection of seven separate spiritual teachings designed for you to learn to align yourself with the circle of life, until the day you leave this world. Each chapter in this book is based upon your life's process. It should not be misinterpreted as repeating itself.

Learning Journey on the Red Road is a book written by an Indian for Indians. The psychology of this way may not apply to the eastern or western way of life, but this is the way of North America. It applies here. And so, my brothers and sisters of European, African or Asian descent, I urge you to use this psychology if you want to attain the holistic way of this island. But as you read what I have written, remember that spirituality here in North America is not a religion. It is a way of life. Remember that the laws of this island should not be altered or added onto in any way. If you're going to judge this book by your own values, then I suggest that you don't read any further.

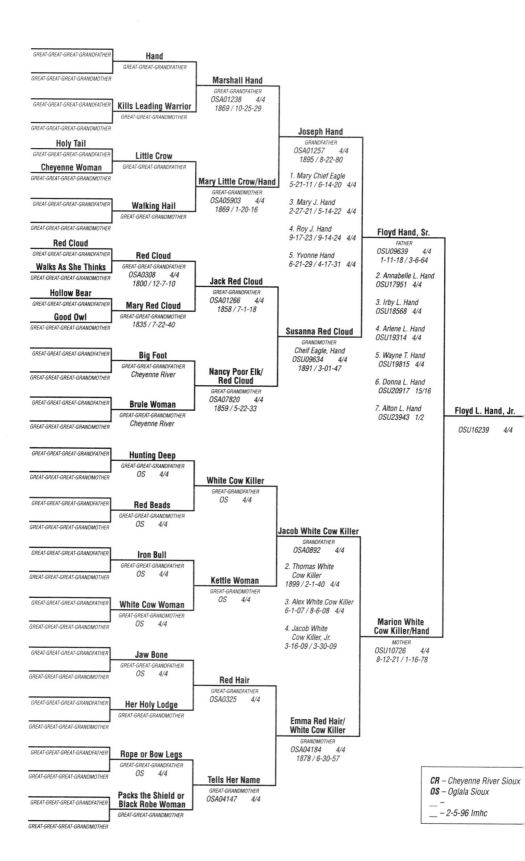

GREAT-GREAT-GREAT-GRANDFATHER | **Hand**
GREAT-GREAT-GRANDFATHER

GREAT-GREAT-GREAT-GRANDMOTHER

GREAT-GREAT-GREAT-GRANDFATHER | **Kills Leading Warrior**
GREAT-GREAT-GRANDMOTHER

GREAT-GREAT-GREAT-GRANDMOTHER

Marshall Hand
GREAT-GRANDFATHER
OSA01238   4/4
1869 / 10-25-29

Holy Tail
GREAT-GREAT-GREAT-GRANDFATHER | **Little Crow**
Cheyenne Woman | GREAT-GREAT-GRANDFATHER
GREAT-GREAT-GREAT-GRANDMOTHER

GREAT-GREAT-GREAT-GRANDFATHER | **Walking Hail**
GREAT-GREAT-GRANDMOTHER

GREAT-GREAT-GREAT-GRANDMOTHER

Mary Little Crow/Hand
GREAT-GRANDMOTHER
OSA05903   4/4
1869 / 1-20-16

Joseph Hand
GRANDFATHER
OSA01257   4/4
1895 / 8-22-80

1. Mary Chief Eagle
5-21-11 / 6-14-20   4/4

3. Mary J. Hand
2-27-21 / 5-14-22   4/4

4. Roy J. Hand
9-17-23 / 9-14-24   4/4

5. Yvonne Hand
6-21-29 / 4-17-31   4/4

Red Cloud
GREAT-GREAT-GREAT-GRANDFATHER | **Red Cloud**
Walks As She Thinks | GREAT-GREAT-GRANDFATHER
GREAT-GREAT-GREAT-GRANDMOTHER | OSA0308   4/4
Hollow Bear | 1800 / 12-7-10
GREAT-GREAT-GREAT-GRANDFATHER | **Mary Red Cloud**
Good Owl | GREAT-GREAT-GRANDMOTHER
GREAT-GREAT-GREAT-GRANDMOTHER | 1835 / 7-22-40

Jack Red Cloud
GREAT-GRANDFATHER
OSA01266   4/4
1858 / 7-1-18

GREAT-GREAT-GREAT-GRANDFATHER | **Big Foot**
GREAT-GREAT-GRANDFATHER | Cheyenne River
GREAT-GREAT-GREAT-GRANDMOTHER

GREAT-GREAT-GREAT-GRANDFATHER | **Brule Woman**
GREAT-GREAT-GRANDMOTHER | Cheyenne River
GREAT-GREAT-GREAT-GRANDMOTHER

**Nancy Poor Elk/
Red Cloud**
GREAT-GRANDMOTHER
OSA07820   4/4
1859 / 5-22-33

Susanna Red Cloud
GRANDMOTHER
Chief Eagle, Hand
OSU09634   4/4
1891 / 3-01-47

Floyd Hand, Sr.
FATHER
OSU09639   4/4
1-11-18 / 3-6-64

2. Annabelle L. Hand
OSU17951   4/4

3. Irby L. Hand
OSU18568   4/4

4. Arlene L. Hand
OSU19314   4/4

5. Wayne T. Hand
OSU19815   4/4

6. Donna L. Hand
OSU20917 15/16

7. Alton L. Hand
OSU23943   1/2

Floyd L. Hand, Jr.

OSU16239   4/4

GREAT-GREAT-GREAT-GRANDFATHER | **Hunting Deep**
GREAT-GREAT-GRANDFATHER
OS   4/4
GREAT-GREAT-GREAT-GRANDMOTHER

GREAT-GREAT-GREAT-GRANDFATHER | **Red Beads**
GREAT-GREAT-GRANDMOTHER
OS   4/4
GREAT-GREAT-GREAT-GRANDMOTHER

White Cow Killer
GREAT-GRANDFATHER
OS   4/4

GREAT-GREAT-GREAT-GRANDFATHER | **Iron Bull**
GREAT-GREAT-GRANDFATHER
OS   4/4
GREAT-GREAT-GREAT-GRANDMOTHER

GREAT-GREAT-GREAT-GRANDFATHER | **White Cow Woman**
GREAT-GREAT-GRANDMOTHER
OS   4/4
GREAT-GREAT-GREAT-GRANDMOTHER

Kettle Woman
GREAT-GRANDMOTHER
OS   4/4

Jacob White Cow Killer
GRANDFATHER
OSA0892   4/4

2. Thomas White
Cow Killer
1899 / 2-1-40   4/4

3. Alex White Cow Killer
6-1-07 / 8-6-08   4/4

4. Jacob White
Cow Killer, Jr.
3-16-09 / 3-30-09

GREAT-GREAT-GREAT-GRANDFATHER | **Jaw Bone**
GREAT-GREAT-GRANDFATHER
OS   4/4
GREAT-GREAT-GREAT-GRANDMOTHER

GREAT-GREAT-GREAT-GRANDFATHER | **Her Holy Lodge**
GREAT-GREAT-GRANDMOTHER
GREAT-GREAT-GREAT-GRANDMOTHER

Red Hair
GREAT-GRANDFATHER
OSA0325   4/4

GREAT-GREAT-GREAT-GRANDFATHER | **Rope or Bow Legs**
GREAT-GREAT-GRANDFATHER
OS   4/4
GREAT-GREAT-GREAT-GRANDMOTHER

GREAT-GREAT-GREAT-GRANDFATHER | **Packs the Shield or
Black Robe Woman**
GREAT-GREAT-GREAT-GRANDMOTHER

Tells Her Name
GREAT-GRANDMOTHER
OSA04147   4/4

**Emma Red Hair/
White Cow Killer**
GRANDMOTHER
OSA04184   4/4
1878 / 6-30-57

**Marion White
Cow Killer/Hand**
MOTHER
OSU10726   4/4
8-12-21 / 1-16-78

GREAT-GREAT-GREAT-GRANDMOTHER

CR – Cheyenne River Sioux
OS – Oglala Sioux
__ –
__ – 2-5-96 lmhc

Introduction

A few years ago I attended a gathering of the Gray Eagle Society, a circle of elders representing the Treaty Council, where I asked permission to speak about hunting rights. According to tradition, I was required to have the age of wisdom in order for my voice to be heard at this council. Although I was an elder at the time, I was considered, at the age of fifty-five, to be too young to speak. So one of the elders stood up and gave me fifteen years of his life, so that I would be eligible to talk. I am a young elder, yet I still have respect for my teachers. Therefore, I want to begin by acknowledging the elders and asking their permission to speak.

The traditionalists who are respected all have an Indian name - a spirit name, which is their identity. My spirit name is Pte Ole - Looks for Buffalo. I am an Oglala Sioux Lakota interpreter from Pine Ridge, South Dakota - the full-blooded grandson of Chief Red Cloud and White Cow Killer, a Cheyenne Oglala Lakota. I come from the family of Red Cloud and the Crazy Horse Band of the Cheyenne Oglala and go many generations back to my grandfather, Big Foot (Poor Elk), who was killed at Wounded Knee. As Sun Dance helper, I serve the sacred circle of the Sun Dance, a ceremony that has been passed down through six generations. My grandfather, William Spotted Crow, was the original caretaker of the Sun Dance. Today, I share this honor with my uncle, James Dubray.

I was born in 1939. As the first-born in the planned marriage of the Red Cloud and Crazy Horse bands, I was recognized by the elders, who gave me a second name - Spotted Moose. And I was honored by my grandmothers Susanna Hand Red Cloud and Emma White Cow Killer. A big celebration was held. They fed the people and horses were given away. Being the first-born, my feet were not allowed to touch the ground for one year after I came into this world. I was one of the very few who had moccasins with beaded soles. And, as I grew up, I started to learn the traditional way that I must live.

At the age of nine I became very sick. After spending a long time in the hospital without getting well, the doctors finally gave up hope and released me, and I was taken home to die. My grandfather James Little Killer (from the Cheyenne Oglala side), who's medicine name was Owl, came and doctored me and said that I would be well. He told me that, upon his death, I was to take his place and walk with the Bear Medicine.

From that time on, I was encouraged to serve the Great Spirit and brought up in a traditional manner by my grandmothers and grandfathers.

Spirit men like George Plenty Wolf, Willie Wounded, Dawson Has No Horse, Frank Young Man Afraid of His Horses, Charlie Red Cloud, Felix Green and Martin High Bear inspired me on this road as I prayed with them. They taught me to humble myself and walk with great respect for the Creator. They told me many stories about the star people and about the change that was to come. They told me stories about the coming of our neighbors, and that some day they were going to try to understand our ways, because we are one blood of all nations - black, red, yellow, white.

Like so many of my people, I grew up confused. We came from parents who were raised in the boarding school days - beaten down and their identities taken away. I had attitude problems and I was very rebellious. The priests used to hit me behind the knees to make me kneel down, but they could never get me on my knees to pray. (This may be why I am suffering with my knees to this day.) I was angry and I became a racist against my own white brothers. That was when my learning began. I was taught that the Great Spirit gave us our destiny and through that, as children, we were hurt. It was not our fault. It was nobody's fault. I was taught that the Great Spirit loves us - he does not scold us, he does not slap us and he does not tell us that we are no good. And as time passed, I came to understand that we are all equal - everything that flies, walks, crawls, two-leggeds - our blood is the same.

My grandfather, Frank Young Man Afraid of His Horses, encouraged me to learn and keep the traditional way of life. In 1954, he told me that one day I would witness something no one had ever seen before - the return of the White Buffalo Calf Lady, the image of the Blessed Virgin Mary - and that I was to be her messenger. That day came. She told me that the time has come for all the people of this world to come together to the heartbeat of Mother Earth - to respect each other and all the things that the Creator has given us - so that some day we may become of one mind, one heart, and one spirit.

We, the Indian people, never lost our spirituality because we were given laws - the seven ritual laws - to guide our lives. We are the wealthiest people in this whole world. We have our diamonds in the sky. We have abundance of food. We are peaceful people. And you will never find a millionaire Indian because, if we have money, we share it all. We have known for hundreds of years that some day our white brothers were going to come to us. Our teachings told us that we must teach them the right way, with wisdom and respect, because our blood is one.

I strongly believe that these teachings must survive for generations to come. We must put our minds together as one, because our blood is one. And if we are to study these holistic rituals of nature's way, we must start from the beginning and not desecrate ourselves in our journey on Mother Earth. The reverse psychology that we were brought up with as Indian people comes from the original belief that a holistic culture goes counter-clockwise. It balances and harmonizes the universe. People today have lost sight of the principles of a beautiful way of life and have instead adopted thirty pieces of silver. We are destroying what we were to protect in favor of the "666". And yet, a lot of people in the last twenty years have found the holistic way in the Indian way. It attracts them because there is discipline and sternness with love, there is a commitment for life, and there is no consciousness of other nationalities. I believe that the hippies almost found it back in the 60's. But they entertained themselves with "loco weed" - marijuana - and never found it.

Spiritual interpreters, or "medicine men" as we are called, have been around among my people since the beginning of time. In the Lakota way, every spiritual interpreter faces twenty-eight years of learning - as the circle of life is seven years in each direction - to defend against the dark forces. A spiritual interpreter has chosen his vocation from early childhood. He walks from one world to another. He talks to the spirits, and they help him to help people. He understands the difference between right and wrong, wrong and right. He understands the destiny of life - that he must get up and continue what he has to do, because this day is gone tomorrow. And he understands that the destiny of life meets up with destination - whether it is life or death.

Over the past twenty-three years, I have traveled to all four directions of the globe teaching and helping people. I have run into a lot of people who are spiritually and morally bankrupt. Insecurities have developed in their minds today. They have a false image of themselves. They are shame-based. They never had T.L.C. - tender loving care - from their fathers and mothers. They don't know their ancestors - their grass roots - and they are not OK. That is why they travel many miles from where they live to join us in Vision Quest and Sun Dance, and try to understand the circle of life.

The greatest medicine we holistic people have is T.L.C. and compassion for our youth. But today, our generation of tomorrow has been forgotten and blamed. We parents are not fulfilling what our purpose in life should be - to set a good example and attitude for our children - because our parents never taught us about T.L.C. They never prepared us for parenthood. We as parents must remember that there are no failures and no mistakes in our journey of life - only examples and hard knocks that we must learn from. And all of us, regardless of our culture, race or nationality, need to find our roots and be proud of our ancestors.

I believe that it is important for people to write books about themselves - their personal life, their deeds and accomplishments. But, too often, they have neglected to write about the traditional way of the Indian people. And nothing has been done for our children - the beginning of life to the end of life. This is why the focus of *Learning Journey on the Red Road* is to bring awareness to the young generation that they must retrieve themselves from the captive mentality that was created for them. By reading this book, I hope that they regain the pride and direction of the Seven Fires, so that they may align themselves to the rituals of life that are part of the circle of life, and refrain from what happened when they were neglected in their youth. The stories that I was taught were given to me to deliver to the people. Therefore, I feel that it is time that we educate ourselves and learn the different rituals and the way we must walk this earth.

Learning Journey on the Red Road is very important for all of us. It is based upon the history of the Indian people in North America. It is not a story. It is a procedure - a circle of life - that can be used in schools or by anyone who wants to attain a higher level of learning. Although some of the ways I talk about here may not apply to all tribes in North America, it is important to know that my people, the Lakota, are the caretakers of the Sacred Pipe that was given to all of us here on this island. We, the Lakota, never surrendered our spirituality. We shared it with all our Indian brothers. And so, today, every tribe on this continent practices our traditional ways. The Drum, the Medicine Wheel, the Sweat Lodge, the Vision Quest and the Sun Dance - all these teachings have come through the Sacred Pipe to be passed on to all the tribes and people of this earth, so that we may come back as one nation. We can all become "Wolakota" - a brotherhood of one mind, heart and spirit - if we respect one another and learn from one another.

Everyone is welcome to walk the Red Road. Use this book as a guide. You can appease your analytical mind as you prepare yourself with this spiritual path. You will be stronger and you will achieve a lot of things. And there are no boundaries for what you can do in life, in your vocation. You will learn not to give up so easily. And you will learn not to be so sensitive, because sensitivity is one of our greatest enemies. There are no failures and there are no mistakes on our journey. You may fall down today, but you get up and start again.

Remember, the one thing that no one can ever take away from you is your spirit, because you cannot take anything that you cannot see.

Chapter 1: The Seven Fires

The teachings of the Sacred Pipe tell us that, in times gone by, seven major prophets came to the Red Nation. Each prophet left the people a prediction of what the future would bring. Each of these prophecies was called a fire and each of these fires referred to a particular period or era of time. Thus, the teachings of the seven prophets are called the Seven Fires.

The ***First Fire*** told of a Red Nation that would rise and follow the spiritual ways of the Sacred Pipe. These traditional ways would be a source of great strength and would rally all the Red people.

The ***Second Fire*** predicted that the Red Nation would be camped by many rivers. At this time, the direction of the sacred ways would be lost. A religion would be born to point the way back to traditional ways, showing the direction to the Sacred Mountain where much rebirth of the religious beliefs occurred.

The ***Third Fire*** said that the Red Nation would find the path to their chosen ground - a land in the west to which they must move their families.

The ***Fourth Fire*** foretold the coming of the light-skinned race.

The ***Fifth Fire*** predicted a great struggle to come.

The ***Sixth Fire*** said that during this time, grandsons and granddaughters would turn against their elders and the spiritual ways would almost disappear.

The ***Seventh Fire*** spoke of the emergence of a new Red Nation - a nation that would retrace its steps to find what it left by the trail. Old flames would be re-kindled and the drum would once again sound its voice. At this time the light-skinned people would be given a choice. If they were to choose the right road, then the Seventh Fire would light the ***Eighth Fire*** - an eternal fire of peace, love and brotherhood. If the light-skinned race would make the wrong choice of roads, then the destruction which they brought with them to this Red Nation would come back to them and cause them much suffering and death.

We the Indian people of North America have hunted and fished on this continent since the beginning of time. My nomadic ancestors followed the seasonal patterns of the buffalo and wild game, which roamed freely across the Great Central Plains. Our woodland tribes lived their lives according to the seasons, catching fish and harvesting rice and berries, so they would have plenty to eat in the cold winter months. Like the game they hunted and the food they harvested, the Indian people knew of no boundaries as we know them today. They were the inhabitants of one great land which they called Turtle Island.

Contrary to popular belief, the Indian people were part of a great North American civilization. Each tribe had its own language and culture. Each tribe had its own traditional methods of healing, learning, teaching, shelter-building, hunting and harvesting. And in each tribe there were well-organized systems of justice, politics, religion and social order. In Lakota society, the main group of tribal leadership was the "Men's Council". Instead of one "chief", there were several leaders in the tribe, each with his own responsibilities. It was their job to make sure that the people were well-fed and protected. The "Medicine Chief" or "Counselor" made sure that his people's physical and spiritual needs were taken care of. The "War Chief" - a soldier/ policeman of the "Tokala" or Kitfox society - was chosen to keep order and protect the community. The "Hunting Chief" was responsible for feeding the people. And in the tribe there was also a "Camp Chief", a "Speaking Chief" and a "Decision Chief".

The Red Nation were a great people. They had a unique perception of the world around them, and an instinctive sense of what is good. To the North American Indian, the most important things in life were:

1. Great Spirit (God), as I understand the circle of life - the great and holy power that is above everything. The Great Spirit made us in order to have mercy upon us. He is good and looks after us.

2. Myself - as I am. The Indian had a deep sense of pride in himself. He saw himself as being extremely important because he was free and he could do difficult things without showing fear or running away from them.

3. My Fellow Man - as he is. He shared with his fellow man and helped him. This made for a strong people.

4. The World (Mother Earth) - the way it is. The Indian people regarded the whole world - the sky, the stars, the sun, the rain, the trees,the animals and the birds - as all one and related. Because the Great Spirit was in everything, the world was revered and considered holy.

On the spiritual road of life, the North American Indians recognized that there were six directions, each with its own powers and special properties, which guided their lives. These directions began with the West.

West - The West is the source of rain and water, which is used for purification in the Sweat Lodge. Water gives us renewed life, release from ignorance of our ways, and personal growth. The West is also the home of the powerful Thunder Being who flies in the midst of thunderstorms in the form of a huge bird. His wings produce thunder, and lightning flashes from his eyes. It is this being who stands against evil and who makes certain that the Sacred Pipe is protected. Each direction is associated with the sacred stone of a specific color; that of the West is black. Each of the directions has a messenger; that of the West is the black thunderbird. The Horse People live here.

North - Winter's home is in the North. Its power promotes good health and growth. Those who misbehave look to it for correction and the wisdom needed to walk the straight path again. It is a challenging power and it promotes endurance (not being controlled). The sacred stone of the North is red, so it has special meaning for the red people and the red power. The North is the home of the White Buffalo Calf Lady and the Buffalo People. Its messenger is the bald eagle.

East - The power of the East is closely associated with the sun. It is here that the sun rises to bring light and enlightenment to all of creation. The path of the sun is from the East to the West. It is thought of as a clockwise direction - the way of the four-leggeds and the wingeds. We two-leggeds walk counter-clockwise. Together we balance each other and harmonize. The morning star is in the East. It is the star of wisdom and new beginnings - a source of inner peace - and it is closely related to the sun. The East is the home of the Elk People. The sacred stone is yellow and its messenger is the brown eagle.

South - The sacred power of the South is connected to life after death and thus it directs people as they walk toward that awesome place. Life begins in the South. Nourishment of every kind comes from there. Warmth and happiness are associated with the power of the South. It is home to the Animal People. The sacred stone is white and the messenger is the white crane.

It is believed that the powers of the directions work only for good, although they may find it necessary to accomplish this good in a different way. They may take the time to discipline those whom they love in order to bring them to their senses and to a more receptive and responsible manner of life.

Great Spirit (Heaven) - The Lakota people think of the heavens as the dwelling place of God. Therefore, they pray to him with the Sacred Pipe by holding its stem up in his direction after they have prayed to the four horizontal directions. He is called "Grandfather" rather than "Father", and "Great Spirit" because he is a spirit. He is the creator of the universe. He is eternal and everything belongs to him. Thus, he is above all other spirits and powers. It is the Grandfather who assigns positions and empowers the other spirits. His knowledge and goodness are perfect and he is the author of the truth. The Red Road walked by mankind leads to him. Since he oversees all things, his help is requested in and through all things. The color blue represents the Great Spirit.

Mother Earth - Mother Earth was made by God and he watches over her now. Men pray to her with the Sacred Pipe because their bodies come from her. She is in us and nourishes all living things. Within her, all created things are related. By praying to her, unity is achieved. The color of Mother Earth is green.

The Six Directions

Great Spirit (above)
Creator of the Universe
Above all other Spirits and Powers
Source of Perfect Knowledge, Goodness and Truth
Overseer of All Things
Color: Blue

North
Source of Health and Control
Home of White Buffalo Calf Lady
Sacred Stone Color: Red
Messenger: Bald Eagle

West
Source of Rain and Water
Home of Thunder Being
Sacred Stone Color: Black
Messenger:
Black Thunderbird

Mother Earth
Created by the Great Spirit,
who Watches over Her
Source of All Living Things
Symbol of Unity and
Relativity
Color: Green

East
Source of Wisdom and
Understanding
Home of Elk People
Sacred Stone Color: Yellow
Messenger: Brown Eagle

South
Source of Life and Destiny
Home of Animal People
Sacred Stone Color: White
Messenger: White Crane

One day, as was predicted by the Fourth Fire, the white people came to North America from Europe, bringing with them their own values and beliefs. They forced many tribes away from their homelands. Because of this forced migration, tribes that were once friendly to one another now fought each other over territorial rights. From the 1600's to the 1850's, during the time of the Fifth Fire, the once friendly tribes, influenced by the white people and their governments, had constant warfare with each other. And later on, to make matters worse for the Indian people, the United States and Canada established a boundary called the "Medicine Line", which cut into their traditional hunting and fishing grounds.

My grandfather Red Cloud recognized the troubles to come, and he said to his people, "The greatest humiliation that we will go through as Indian people is to lay down our arms to see beyond the horizon, from where our generation of grandchildren is going to come. If we do not make peace, we will stand separately and we will be weak as a nation. Today, I lay down my weapon in front of my wife and my grandchildren for I, Red Cloud, pray that we work together so that we may take the good out of our relatives and use it. And we will give the goodness of ourselves to them."

And so, the Indian people tried to make peace. At first, the white governments pledged to protect our territorial rights and sovereignty with promises and treaties. As they broke these promises one at a time, the Indian people were forced to take stand after stand in order to renew their aboriginal rights and claim the protection of the original treaties. The governments responded by rejecting their claims without any serious consideration, passing them off as myth or confused tradition. These opinions, in turn, made their way into written history, to be taught in schools. (So, to this day, Indian people are viewed as political refugees or immigrants within their own country, where they were once free to move about.)

Today, the Indian people of North America are acknowledged to be either United States citizens, Canadian citizens or Indians as defined by the Indian Act, yet we are officially denied aboriginal rights in the countries where we live. And we are often denied our role in North American history, which is conveniently so compatible with the social policy of today. The governments of both the United States and Canada have failed to meet their responsibilities to the Indian people. They continue to let us down despite our pleas.

We the Indian people once had a way of life. This way of life was destroyed with the coming of the white man. It is hard to say at which point in time we abandoned our aboriginality here in North America. The real truth is buried under the devastation caused by the assimilation policies of federal governments. The original intent of these policies was to protect the Indian people from the unscrupulous actions and exploitation of commercial interests. But gradually, they made their way into our reservations and became part of a plan to assimilate us into mainstream North American society.

The plan was tailor-made to the European way of thinking. But the results took a cruel twist, and they became the shame of both the United States and Canadian governments. Now, each year, we see more and more of our children handed over to the care of Children's Aid Societies, where they are abused and neglected. Each year, we see more of our people becoming dependent on welfare and our relatives and young people addicted to alcohol and drugs. Look at our reservations today, and you see third world countries in a critical state of social breakdown, with levels of poverty, disease, violence and anti-social behavior far above those in the average North American community.

What are the root causes of the problems in our Indian society today? Well, supposing a male and female wolf were captured and confined to a zoo. If by some miracle they escaped, they would automatically, by instinct, know how to survive. However, if they didn't escape and eventually had young cubs, these wolf cubs would be born in captivity. As they grew up, the cubs would be dependent on the zoo-keepers to feed them. They would grow up never realizing who they really were. Their wolfness would only be skin deep and their natural survival instincts would be gone. A new breed of wolf would be created, marking the beginning of a captive generation of wolves.

And so, a new breed of Indian began to emerge on Indian reservations. This was - and still is to this day - what I call the "captive generation". Like the wolf cub raised in captivity, the true characteristics of the reservation Indian are only skin deep. He is heavily dependent on his keepers. His natural survival instincts - ingenuity, creativity and individuality - were never allowed to flourish. Instead, he became the scorn of American society. Those of us who were raised traditionally were greatly shunned back in the 1950's and 1960's. They called us "red niggers". The signs in the cafes read, "Dogs and Indians not allowed." Yet we had known for hundreds of years that some day our white brothers were going to come to us. And we were told that we must teach them the right way.

It was back in the early 1970's that Indianism began to march backwards. As was foretold by the Sixth Fire, a lot of our people did not want to be known as Indians. They didn't want to have Indian names. They didn't want to have anything to do with the Sacred Pipe and they rejected the traditional ways. They stopped thinking of the Indian as a beautiful person with braided hair. They forgot that they had a code of ethics. They stopped studying the purity of the heart, mind and spirit. They forgot that they had spiritual power and a spiritual guide, and that they had dignity. They forgot that they should have great respect for their mother, their sister and their daughter, and the highest honor for their grandmother. And they forgot that the Indian lady walked in respect - in a dress, with braided hair. A lot of our Indian ladies didn't want to be like that. They would rather wear fancy three-piece suits and high heels, and deny that they were related to the full-bloods.

But despite what was going on, three Indian nations - the Cheyenne, the Arapaho and the Sioux - managed to maintain their code of ethics and keep their spiritual principles intact. Then in 1973 at Wounded Knee my tribe, the Oglala Sioux, got an opportunity to voice our needs and stand up for what we believed in, and we became very popular as Indian people. It was the beginning of the time of the Seventh Fire. Our great teachers and leaders - Crazy Horse, Red Cloud, Sitting Bull, Kills White Buffalo - were once again remembered. And a lot of tribes began to borrow and imitate the Lakota ways - the traditional dances, the roots, the eagle feathers, the eagle staff, and the eagle whistle. Yet, while some tribes borrowed our ways, many despised the Lakota because we knew who we were. We were the only tribe that ever took the flag away from the United States - at Little Big Horn. That is why we have the right to that American flag. We can hang it for window curtains and use it to make shirts or blankets, because we took it away. It is ours.

In 1975, my elders told me that I was an Ojibway spirit - of Ojibway descent - named "Spotted Moose", and so I was to go to Canada to bring back the traditional ways to the people there. The Ojibways of Wabagoon and the Midewinin both knew I was coming. Back in 1933 they were told that a young man was going to go through their land building fires. And so, for the next seven years, I traveled through Canada building Sweat Lodges, running ceremonies and teaching the ways of the drum. One day I visited an elder in Dakota country, near Winnipeg, Manitoba. He was laying there with a grandma sitting beside him, getting ready to go home. This elder said to me, "Before I go, I would like to see my children have a pow-wow. I would like to see a big pow-wow arbor here. I would like to hear them sing." So I doctored him and sat him up, and two years later we had one of the biggest Dakota pow-wows in Manitoba. And he was there, smiling. Five years later, he went home. That elder had given up. He thought he would never see the return of our sacred ways.

But as I went through Canada teaching the sacred ways, the Royal Canadian Mounted Police (RCMP) were right behind me. The young generation all came. As soon as I taught them how to run the lodge, I took off and the RCMP raided that place. But I kept going until 1982, when they finally caught me. The Mounties and their government tried to stop me because they were provoked by the spirituality that I carried for the people. I had to go through these ways because of my elders.

My worst battle back then was with the Catholic church. "This heathen, where does he come from? He's got horns on," they said to the people. Finally, we had it out in Eagle Lake, Ontario. Just a few years later, in 1985, as a gesture of reconciliation with the Christian faith, I was asked by the bishop of St. Paul's Cathedral in Minnesota to say a few words after mass. So I said to the bishop, "I'll tell you what, I'm not just going to say a few words. I'm going to say the mass." He agreed, so I put my medicine blanket on - my feathers, the whole shebang - and I came in to say the mass. The drum began to play, the voices sang, the whole cathedral echoed, and everybody in that jam-packed cathedral started to cry. I said, "Tunkasila, thank you," because of all the time I was beaten up in that Catholic church. I was able to perform the mass and unite everybody together. And I believe from that day on, many priests began coming to the Sweat Lodge, because they realized that we are all one nation.

Following the uprising at Wounded Knee, a new breed of Indian came into focus. I call him the "Wahoo" - the born-again Indian warrior. He wore braids and a choker, and walked with a beautiful blonde wearing dark glasses by his side. Now the Indian lady wanted to rediscover her Indian roots by bringing her European respect back to her culture. She wanted to wear the pants. But she forgot that a true traditional Indian lady does not speak out above the man. She does not try to be a leader or a medicine person. She knows her place. And she does not have to suffer, because the Great Spirit has given her the honor of being the total force of a nation.

Today it is these "born-again Wahoos" - these intellectual Indians who were never brought up in a traditional way - who rule the newspapers and media, claiming to be the spokespeople for all Indians, always critical of everything and always accusing others of stealing their ways. What they don't realize is that you can't steal anything that is given and you can't sell anything that you can't see. A lot of tribes have laid claim to what is given from God. That is not the way it should be. The Medicine Wheel, the Dream Catcher, the Sweat Lodge, the Sun Dance, the Vision Quest, and the teachings have all come through the Sacred Pipe to be passed out to the tribes and the people of this earth, so that we come back as one nation. It is important for each and every one of us.

It is a sad reality today that the Indian who once mastered the tools needed to maintain his way of life is now controlled by his tools. He is the product of an outside society that determines his self-image, totally at the mercy of tools and natural resources controlled by others. He is denied the opportunity to enrich his environment with the fruits of his vision of self-defined labor. This denial leads to a rapid loss of his self-worth, which in turn destroys every aspect of his supportive culture.

In the last twenty years, intensive programs have been introduced to solve our problems. The Medical Services Branch of the United States government brought in a program called "Devolution" which, like other federal service programs, advocated eventual Indian control. But these programs are only sugar-coated pills. In reality, they are extensions of the federal bureaucracy and they're all basically the same. They are designed to deal with the symptoms and ignore the causes. The government recognizes many issues but has no strategy to deal with them. If Indian self-government is ever to succeed, there must be an evaluation of our communities and long-term social, economic and educational planning, with the overall goal of improving the quality of life for all reservation residents.

My purpose here on this earth during the time of the Seventh Fire is to bring the culture, the identity and the traditional respect back to the elders and back to our Indian society so that we can live in both cultures without the need of alcohol and drugs in our lives. Today, our children are turning to drug and alcohol use within our schools and homes at an alarming rate and many of them are dying young through suicide and violence. This is happening because they have lost their identity and their self-respect. One of the last things my great-grandfather, Red Cloud, talked about before he died was the "black road". He said that if we do not teach our children what we know, then they will be squashed like frogs on that black road. He was talking about alcoholism.

Our children have forgotten themselves and they walk in pain. They never had a grandfather to talk to them. Nor did they have a father to wipe their tears when they were hurt. This world that the European culture has created is so regimented that it is an unhappy place to live in. Everything is forced upon you - Christianity, education, numbers, regulations, curfews - and as soon as you turn eighteen, you either have to pay something back to stay in the house or you have to move out. You are always paying for something. You do not have the free will to stay with your mother and father as long as you want. It is really a cold society.

They are a beautiful people, this young generation. They did not ask to come here. As young children, they have no control over what happened to them in the place where they were born. They are here because, just like you and I, they have a journey to fulfill. We were taught that we are the caretakers of everything in this world, including the children. The Creator has given our children to us on loan so that we may help them grow up. They are not ours. And it is up to us to teach them the right way.

In the traditional, holistic Indian way, we knew how to live with each other because our children learned from their grandmothers and grandfathers in the home. Our children were taught their history and they were told stories to prepare them for womanhood or manhood. And now, for the benefit of our children, we Indian people must return to our traditional ways. In our teachings, we revere the sacred bald eagle, the grandmother, as the supreme law of this island. Just as the eagle parents prepare their young to leave the nest, it is up to us to prepare our children with the skills, the knowledge and all the things they will need to have in their lives. To do this, we must look to our cultural and spiritual ways.

We must care about our children. We must be stern with them, but we must never neglect them. The most important thing that I as an Indian man can give to my children is my attitude and example, and my time. When they want to talk to me, I just listen, so they can talk. I will always spend time with them in order to learn from them. You have a beautiful voice that your children listen to. You don't need to abuse them. Everything that we instill in a child is what they are going to become. If the young man sees his father abusing his mother, he too is going to grow up and abuse his companion. Our children's behavior is the mirror of our behavior. Knowing this, I realize how important it is for each Indian man to be responsible for his family. So, in order to fulfill the need to build a strong and balanced life, I will break the cycle of hurt to ensure a good Indian way of life, as mental health is important to our children and our generations to come, which are not yet born.

As an Indian man, I will always look at my priorities. The Great Spirit gave me my family and he has given me this time to spend to be a teacher in my own family. This family is a place for all the teachings that have been handed down from generation to generation. And in turn, it is the teachings of my grandparents that I must hand down to the next generation. I will always nurture our family's spiritual, cultural and social life. I will teach my children to pray at every meal and smudge our house with sage every morning and every evening - in respect to the Great Spirit for everything he has given us. I will pray in my own language to help my children learn the sacred songs and dances. I will demonstrate trust, respect and honor - how to receive visitors by giving them something to eat and drink. And I will never give up this life to leave my family only to the mother. I will always be there to restore the strength of my family. These are the ways that my elders have talked about.

It is very easy for the children to go astray in today's world. But I will work to provide positive alternatives for them. I will talk to them and teach them our way of life - the peace, love and harmony. I will encourage them to get an education. I will encourage them to get involved in sports. I will always encourage them to talk to their elders for guidance. Mostly, I will try to be a role model myself. I make this commitment to my children on the sacred mountain, so that they will have the courage to find guidance in the traditional spiritual ways.

I will teach my children that the source of life, Mother Earth, gives us plants, the four-leggeds, the wingeds and the human beings. Mother Earth is the greatest teacher we have. If we listen to her and respect her, we will live in harmony with her. She will recycle the things we consume and make them available to our children and to their children. We as Indian men must always teach our children how to care for Mother Earth for our future generations. And so, I will treat Mother Earth with honor and respect. I will honor everything she has given to us and to all forms of life. And I will teach my children the natural laws - that Mother Earth is alive and we are here to protect her - so that some day they will carry what I have said in a good way whenever they see someone abusing the earth. This way, the respect for land, water and air will remain intact for our children and their children and their children. The earth does not belong to us. We belong to the earth. We come from the world of darkness from the womb of our mother, and we will once again enter the world of darkness at the time of our death.

I will encourage my children to visit their grandparents and elders in the community, as they play a big role in our culture and our teachings. Without these teachings, I would not be sitting here telling you these stories. I realize that we, the men, and our spiritual companions become the foundation in our family life. My companion tells us what to do and I will show the children what to do. And I will listen to my companion for our family's benefit and for the benefit of our way of life. All you mothers and fathers, I encourage you to love your children. Take time out. Go for walks with them. If there is a spiritual gathering, take your children. Don't leave them at home. They are the ones who are going to survive us. Never leave your children. Wipe their tears. Because a lot of us who are out there grew up without a father or mother. We have that chance here on this Red Road.

Our Indian communities need to be restored to health so that our future generations will be able to live the way we live in our language and culture. Traditionally, the Indian community has provided many things for the "tiosipa" - the family - including a sense of belonging. We must remember that we belong to each other and our relatives. We need to learn to socialize - to visit each other, to be friends, and to hold out our hand and shake hands. We must honor the elders and those who live in pain. And we must show care and compassion for those people in our tiosipa who are suffering from mind changes brought on by alcohol and drugs, because it is only when these things vanish that our community will be free of violence. If we can do all of this, then others will follow. We must be an example for other people. This is the way that we must live.

As Indian people, we must support one another in our communities. If someone is doing something, we should get behind them and support them like our non-Indian brothers do. But as Indians, we behave like crabs. What do I mean by that? Well, it has to do with the Crab Story. A white man and an Indian were gathering crabs. The white man gathered his crabs and he looked in his bucket and saw that the crabs were crawling out in different directions. He looked at the Indian gathering crabs and saw that nothing was coming out of his bucket, so he said to the Indian, "How come your crabs aren't crawling out?" And the Indian replied, "Because they're Indian crabs. Come on over and take a look." So the white man looked in the Indian's bucket and saw that, as one crab started to crawl out, all the other crabs jumped on him and pulled him back down. It's always like that in our Indian culture. When one wants to get ahead, the others always want to bring him down.

And so, as an Indian person - a holistic person - I will try to work to strengthen our community. I will give back to the community where I was raised by donating to the families everything I have achieved for myself in my life. I will feed the families in my community. I will talk to the children. I will be their father, their grandfather and their uncle. And I will never close my door to anyone, because friendship is our support and strength. I will look at all the things I am to do and the decisions I must make on behalf of the next seven generations. This way, our children and grandchildren will live in healthy "tiosipas" - communities.

As a warrior, I realize that we can make no gains without the Great Spirit in our lives. Sometimes I am tempted to give up. But I look at the covenant that I carry for the Great Spirit and I realize that, without the Creator and without the spiritual way of life, life would become meaningless for me. Spirituality is the gift from the Great Spirit for us to carry. This is why I vowed to walk the Red Road. As an Indian man, I will return to the traditional values that I have learned from my ancestors to pass on to future generations. I will also look at the powers of our ceremonies - the religious ways - for they are important to our survival in this land. We have survived for many hundreds of years thanks to our spirituality. It is our way of life, this holistic way of life, that we are teaching our yellow, black and white brothers - to pray each day and to give of themselves instead of always taking.

On this learning journey on the Red Road, we are committed to walk in a spiritual way. As a spiritual man, I'm always trying to dedicate my whole life to this way. I will always try to think of the kind of person I want to be when I'm an elder. I will develop myself now into this person. I will walk with the Great Spirit and the grandfathers at my side. I will always walk and think in a positive way. I will develop a good mind. I will examine myself daily - the good things that I do, the things that I need to improve. I will examine my strengths. I will ask the Great Spirit to help guide me. Each day I have learned, I will listen to the Creator's voice in the wind. I will watch Mother Nature and learn from her lessons on this sacred journey I am making. And I will also look at the principles, which we call the star people in the sky, to guide me as they have guided my ancestors - with dignity and love.

Chapter 2: The White Buffalo Calf Lady

Back in 1954, my grandfather Frank Young Man Afraid of His Horses told me a story. "Grandson," he said, "you see that full moon rising? That's a wean - a woman. Woman is the supreme law of creation for the Indian people. She is the giver of life. The spiritual circle and the universe that has created everything is a woman. She is the sun, she is the moon and she is the earth that we are sitting on. We, the men, have to protect the women. We must provide for them. We must die for them."

Here in North America, the belief of all the Indian people is that the power of this island is the woman. When you come into this country, there is a lady welcoming you - the Statue of Liberty. If you look at the United States flag, you see the power of America - the red people. The seven fires and the seven laws that a lady gave to the red people are written into that flag - the seven stripes. And the six white lines and five-pointed stars represent all the challenges that we face - the dark side that we must learn to understand. The whole circle of life is written into the American flag, and it was a lady named Betsy Ross who made the first one.

If you look at the color of the Canadian flag, you see the power of Canada - the red people. You see the medicine of this country - the maple leaf. And when you look up in the sky, you see the grandmother bald eagle flying between heaven and earth, protecting the nation. Everything here on this island - the four-leggeds, the buffalo, the man, the lady, the medicine and the bear - pertains to the spiritual power of the woman, which is the universe. And everything here teaches us that we were put on this earth for a reason.

Lakota legend says that a very long time ago, there was great hardship and strife in North America. The nations of this island were making war with each other and there was a great famine. And the people prayed for help.

Then one day, two scouts were out looking for buffalo. They came to the top of a high hill and looked north and they saw something coming a long way off. When it came closer they cried out, "It's a woman!" And it was. One of the scouts, being foolish, had bad thoughts about her and spoke them. But the other man, being respectful, replied, "That is a sacred woman. Throw all your bad thoughts away."

As the woman approached the scouts, they saw that she wore a fine buckskin dress. Her hair was long and she was very beautiful. And she knew what both of them were thinking. "You do not know me," she said, "but if you do as you think, then you may come." So the foolish scout went towards the woman and stood before her. Suddenly, a white cloud appeared and covered them. The woman emerged from the cloud and, as it blew away, all that was left of the foolish scout was a skeleton covered in worms.

The respectful man was horrified at what he saw. But the sacred woman looked at him and calmly said, "Go home and tell your people that I am coming. Tell them to build a big tipi for me in the center of the nation." So he went quietly and delivered the message to his people. They did as they were told and they waited in the big tipi for her arrival.

After a while, the sacred woman came. As she entered the tipi, she sang a song:

"With a visible breath I am walking
A voice I am sending as I walk
In a sacred manner I am walking
With visible tracks I am walking
In a sacred manner I walk
I bring you the Sacred Pipe
Carry it with respect, for I am watching
I bring you the sacred laws."

While she sang, a sweet-smelling white cloud came from her mouth and she handed something to the leader of the nation. It was a pipe with a bison calf carved on one side, representing the earth that bears and feeds us. Hanging from the stem were thirteen eagle feathers symbolizing the sky and the thirteen moons. They were tied with a grass that never breaks.

"Behold," said the woman, "I bring you seven laws that are the sacred gift of survival:

Walk quietly.
Help others as you help yourself.
Love people as you would love yourself.
Respect others as you respect yourself.
Set an example for your children.
Hold out your hand and bring everybody together.
Say thank you for your life.

With this Sacred Pipe you shall multiply and be a good nation. Nothing but good shall come of it. Only the hands of the good shall take care of it, and the bad shall never see it."

Then she sang again and walked out of the tipi. As the people watched her leave, she suddenly changed into a white buffalo calf. With a snort, she galloped away and vanished beyond the horizon. And from that time on, there was peace and harmony among the nations once again. The buffalo returned and the people had food and shelter.

Our teachings have told us for many years that the Lady would return when there is once again conflict and hardship in the world. My grandfather told me that the people of the world are being corrupted because they are losing their spirituality. He said that I would witness something that no man had ever seen before - the return of the White Buffalo Calf Lady. He told me to prepare for this time. He said that I would go through life not being respected or trusted. I would go through life not respecting anything, hurting people. I would go through a life of confusion. But he said that within me lives the spirit of the Lady and that some day this would be recognized.

So, as I grew up in Pine Ridge, I got no respect from my tribe, the Oglalas. People didn't think much of me because I walked with shame, hurt and fear as a human being. My grandfather had taught me that, as an Indian man, I was to have the highest honor for my grandmother, my mother, my sister, my daughter and my wife. As a man, I was to stand up for them. But I didn't listen. I was weak and I turned to alcohol.

Then, in 1968, I was lying in my bedroom in my grandmother's house and I saw something shimmering on the wall. It was the outline of a beautiful lady with a flowing rainbow. At first I thought it was just my hangover. But then I realized that the image was real and I got all excited. So the next day, I went to Holy Rosary Mission and told my high school teacher, a Jesuit priest, what I had seen. He said, "Junior, you're hallucinating. They only see the lady in Italy. Indians don't see these holy people." But I knew I saw something that night. And I thought, "Why me?"

Twenty years later, in 1988, when I was living in Minnesota, the image of the lady again appeared on my bedroom wall. This time, it was very clear. She had a smooth, beautiful face and dark, piercing eyes, and she wore a chiffon dress with rainbow colors. She was the most beautiful woman I had ever seen. In the Lakota language, she said to me, "Tell them I am coming." She repeated this message three times.

So there I was, going around telling everybody that she's coming, and they all laughed at me. They thought I was nuts. But then I began to remember the teachings of my grandfathers and grandmothers. I took my Sacred Pipe and I went out among my relatives - my white, yellow and black brothers - to tell them she was coming and that the time of change was here - and I realized that we are all equal because our blood is the same.

Six years passed. In March of 1994, I was leading a prayer ceremony with more than sixty people in Minnesota, and the White Buffalo Calf Lady appeared again. This time, she spoke. She said, "When the cherries are black, I will return and my father will take my place." And she delivered a message to all the people of the world.

She said the colors of the four directions - Red (west), Black (north), Yellow (east) and White (south) - represent the four races of people. Each race was given a covenant to protect:

The Covenant of the Water that runs in our bodies - the blood - and the rivers and lakes of Mother Earth, was given to the yellow people of Asia. They had one long braid from the center of their head and they worshipped a sacred yellow rock called Buddha to care for this blood - the water of life. And they guided their lives by their spiritual beliefs and meditation. But the yellow nation broke their covenant. They started to raise poppies, which they developed into opium and used to contaminate the water in their bodies. This affected Mother Earth and all the waters of this earth became polluted.

The Covenant of the Air was given to the white people of Europe. Described as having straight long hair, this nation worshipped tablets made of white stone which they called the Ten Commandments. They guided their lives through Christianity. But they too violated their covenant by polluting the air we breathe for their own personal gain - with manufacturing, automobiles, airplanes, ozone. And the white brothers became a lost nation when they killed their leader, Jesus. Because of this, they were destined to blend into the people of the yellow, black and red races.

The Covenant of the Fire within our hearts, representing peace, love and harmony among nations, belonged to the black people of Africa. They wore thirteen braids on their head and worshipped Juju (Voodoo) - a black marble rock in the form of a water buffalo calf. Their leader was Mohammed. But the black people also violated their covenant by becoming an angry tribe. They misused that fire that was entrusted to them - our energy force - and began to war with each other, killing brothers and old friends.

The Covenant of the Earth represents our flesh. It was given to the red people of North America. They wore two long braids on their head and they worshipped a Sacred Pipe made of red stone (which, to this day, you can only find in one place - Pipestone, Minnesota). Their spiritual guide was the White Buffalo Calf Lady. And the red people, too, broke their covenant because they became disrespectful to Mother Earth and allowed her to be desecrated through false promises.

There is a reason why every one of these brothers has broken his covenant. That is just the way it has been written in the skies. (It was also written in the Book of Revelations.) But, of all four nations, only the red people have kept the foundations of their spirituality alive - through the seven laws given to them by the Lady hundreds of years ago. The white, yellow and black nations believed that the man was boss because their leaders were all men. And they brought their beliefs and values to this island. Now, spiritually and morally bankrupt, they are coming to the Indian people for guidance and answers. And it is up to us to teach them the right way.

The White Buffalo Calf Lady explained that, because we have broken our covenants, we are destined to endure pain and hardship before we find new peace. Because all four nationalities have violated their responsibilities, she has returned after five hundred years to deliver this message:

1. The power of the woman has returned to lead all nations. It will begin in the east, the home of the yellow race.

2. Destruction and devastation, brought on by natural and man-made disasters, will occur - fires, floods, hurricanes, tornadoes, tidal waves, earthquakes and wars. Cities will be especially hard-hit with natural gas line and electrical catastrophes. A cloud will cover the whole earth for 120 to 140 days.

3. 1997, 1998 and 1999 will be difficult years. Evil will destroy evil. Great famine will occur and many people will die. Governments will be in turmoil. Those now in power will lose their positions and new governments will be formed.

4. In twenty-four years - on the 21st day of the 21st year of the 21st century - peace, love and harmony will return through the guidance of the woman.

5. New nations will restore a new world from the old world. "Tokatakiya Iciskanpo," she said. Prepare for the future.

On August 20, 1994, when the cherries turned black, a female White Buffalo Calf was born on a farm near Janesville, Wisconsin. The owners of the farm, the Heider family, named her "Miracle." When Miracle came, the Blessed Virgin Mary came. Just as Jesus - a star person sent to teach the people - was born in a manger with animals, so the White Buffalo Calf

Lady was born in a manger as a woman. And on that day two eagles, representing the spirit people, came to the Heider farm.

A month later, a great ceremony was held in her honor. About two hundred people from all tribes gathered on the Heider farm to give thanks and pray for peace, harmony and a new beginning for mankind. Television cameras, microphones and reporters were everywhere.

"This day has been a long time coming," I said. "Over the years, we the nations of this world have drifted apart. We have been put on separate islands as a test and now we have been given the biggest test of all - to unite as one people. We all come from the darkness of our mother's womb. In a short time, we will all return to darkness. We have air pollution filling up the skies and our waters are polluted. We have drugs and we're getting heart attacks from unhealthy living. And we have forgotten the responsibility that was given to us. Today, we come together like we are supposed to."

Arvol Looking Horse, the keeper of the original Sacred Pipe that was given to the Lakota people, brought out the pipe and we prayed for world peace. Each member of the Heider family was given gifts from the Indian people, in appreciation for their friendship and their care of the White Buffalo Calf. I said to them, "Your family is our family. We will always be with you in prayer." Then my uncle, James Dubray, offered "spirit food" and put it into the fire, and we all had a great feast. Our teachings told us that the calf would be born to a white family, so that the white people may know about her return. The Heider family was chosen because they are a humble people who care about all things.

And the Heiders were also given a gift in honor of Marvin, the father of the White Buffalo Calf. When the Lady told us she was coming, she said that her father would take her place, meaning that her father would die so that she could live. I had told the Heiders that this was going to happen. In a vision, I saw a big black object in the bull's stomach area. This prophecy was fulfilled when Marvin died just twelve days after the calf was born. A post-mortem showed that he had a large blood clot in his stomach.

Thousands of people of all nationalities from all over the world have visited the White Buffalo Calf, bringing gifts and prayer offerings in her honor. According to her prophecy, the Lady said she would appear as the colors of all the nations - beginning as white, then red, then black, then yellow. And so it happened. The calf was born with a white coat, which turned red, then black and now it's yellow. Eventually she will turn white again, but only if the people of the world come together and start living in harmony. So far, twenty-three eagles have come to the Heider farm. This means that we must wake up. The eagle is a forewarning sign that the destruction of cities is coming.

The power of the woman has returned now. The Lady said it would begin where the waters run to the east - where the yellow people are. And there, in Beijing, the women are coming together. She said that she will cleanse herself through fire, water, earth and air, which will bring about natural and man-made disasters. Just watch the news and look at the floods that are happening today. What do you see? A $200,000 house floating by and, on top of it, the owner trying to save it, hanging on to the chimney. My grandfather would have laughed, because he used to say that only a fool would build a house by a river. The Lady is teaching us that material things are becoming invalid because we have tried to overrule her with our material values. But through these disasters, we will gain awareness.

And the Lady said that all the animals will be wearing all white and all jet black, and they will migrate to the place where they are supposed to be - like in Noah's Ark. You notice that the animals are moving nowadays. The people of the Ojibway nation already know that. Their spiritual guide, the black panther of the north, has returned to North America. We the Indian people have been talking about these things for centuries. But nobody has believed us. And now, it's all happening.

We are cutting too many of our Mother's body hairs - the trees. We are polluting the waters and we are warming the earth. We are taking the lives of more and more four-leggeds and wingeds all the time. All for the sake of a dollar, we are destroying the earth. We are speeding up the earth and beating it up and we're trying to figure out what's going wrong. When I saw the eagle fly above the city, I knew what it meant because I have listened to the prophecies. The Lady said that she will cover all these cities with her blanket and she will shake it. This means earthquakes. An earthquake under water causes the water to rush out. Look at Los Angeles. Look at Toronto. The spirits tell us they will be under water. But we don't listen.

I had a dream once. I was in a city with no people in it - just me, and a silent enemy. This silent enemy was hunting for me. I thought if I could out-smart him, I could catch him before he catches me. I thought about this dream for a long time and I finally realized what that silent enemy was - pollution. And in another dream I saw seven fires burning in a circle.

The people living in that circle were content and lived happy lives. On the outside were people crying and screaming because they couldn't get inside. After many years, I realized what that meant - the circle surrounded by seven fires represented the holistic way of life.

The final journey begins at the turn of the century. "Prepare," the Lady said. Are you ready for the changes? Do you have candles in your home? Do you have a heating stove? Those who don't prepare will be the first to go. And those people who live in high-rise apartments, dependent on heat and electricity - they're the ones who are going to have the hardest time. All the riches in the world are not going to save you. You can have the biggest, most wonderful house in the world, but it's not going to save you. Some people say that we can get energy from the sun. But solar energy is not going to penetrate the contamination of the skies. This whole world is being covered in a blanket of cloud and we're causing it. You look at the sky above the cities in the summer and you see a brownish-gray haze. Learn how to prepare yourself for the changing times that are coming. Learn how to make candles. Have lamps and kerosene ready. Get a wood stove. Gather wood.

Learn how to harvest berries and wild potatoes because you won't be able to run to the store and get some canned goods. They'll be all bought out. And if you think you'll be able to hop in your car and get out of the city in twenty minutes, think again. A million other people are going to be doing the same thing. On the 21st day of the 21st year of the 21st century, you'll look up in the sky and see three stars lined up. That will be the time of the great changes. It won't be the end of the world. Only those people who haven't listened - two billion of us - are going to go. Don't be frightened. Prepare. If you live the holistic way, you're going to survive.

On this island - in the true, traditional way of worship that goes back over 600 years - the supreme law of the universe, as my elders taught me, was the woman and the circle. These teachings came from the sacred ways of the pipe. This is an island of red, yellow, black and white. Here, there is a red stone and the law of the mountains. The rituals and respect belong here. If you were born in North America, you are rooted on this island. You are born under the power of the red stone. You're entitled to that.

Each nation has its beliefs and its own way of speaking. But the Sacred Pipe - the "Canunpa" that the lady brought on this island - belongs on this island. You must learn this way and walk this way here in North America. Christianity belongs in Europe. Juju belongs in Africa. Buddha belongs in Asia. They don't belong here. We all have our respectful places to practice these religions. But if you use your mind spirit and try to combine all these into one, it will not work because you are not initiating the roots of this island.

I am a messenger. I am to spread the word from the great Lady - the White Buffalo Calf Lady, Guadeloupe, Corn Lady, the Blessed Virgin Mary, whatever you want to call her - that the time has come when we must all come together to the heartbeat of Mother Earth, the drum. The journey that we are taking together involves all of us, not just one nationality. It doesn't matter what race or country we're from, we all come from our mother. Every summer, my students come around to South Dakota to take part in the Sun Dance. We have all different nations from all over the world dancing here. It's beautiful. One year there were one hundred and sixty seven dancers from different tribes. We could tell we were coming together in that circle.

Now, all over the world, through the Great Spirit and the Sacred Pipe, we are coming back to the center of the drum, as one. Whether you're black, red, yellow or white, when you put those colors together and mix them up, it's the color of our blood. And this is why we are coming together. Come. Break bread. Hold out your hand.

Tunkasila, Great Spirit, you have blessed us as a nation on this island. You have made our blood as one through the Sacred Pipe. And you have given us a direction to follow, so that we may understand peace, love and harmony as we walk. And Grandmother, you have warned us many times, but we have not listened. Now you have come back to give us a lesson. Grandmother, we want to thank you, because you have brought the power back.

Aho! Mitakuye Oyasin - All My Relations.

Chapter 3: The Teachings of the Elders

One day, my elders told me to go out and look for horses. I had my rope and went over the hill. It was one hundred degrees outside and there I was, standing in the hot sun looking for the horses. Finally, I realized that they must be in the shade where it's cool, so I walked another two miles and, sure enough, there they were under a shady tree. You see, that is how the elders teach you. They teach you how to get rid of yourself. They teach you common sense.

In my tribe, the teachings we received from our elders as young men prepared us for life. As part of our learning, we were told "Iktomi" stories - children's stories that were meant to teach by example. These stories taught us to develop psychology - to be aware of everything around us. One of the stories was about Spider Man - a character who will connive you and fool you.

Spider Story - Spider was walking and he came upon a buffalo skull. As he passed by, he heard a pow-wow going on - drums, singing, dancing. But when he went a little ways past that buffalo skull, the singing stopped. So he turned around and walked past that buffalo skull again, and again he heard the pow-wow going on. So finally, Spider peeked into the eye hole of the buffalo skull and he saw the ant people dancing in there, having a good time. So Spider yelled, "Hey, brothers, I want to join you." But they didn't pay attention to him. So he tried to get inside and, as he pushed his head inside the buffalo skull, all the ants got frightened and ran away in different directions.

Spider tried to get his head out of the buffalo skull, but realized he couldn't. With the buffalo skull stuck on his head, he stood up but he couldn't see where he was going. As he began walking, feeling his way around, he heard water running. And he thought, "Hey, I'm going to soak this buffalo skull and break it open!" So he went down to a river and stuck his head in the water.

As Spider soaked his head, he heard a couple of women talking. "Sister! Let's go this way." So he thought, "Hey, I'm going to fool these ladies." He pulled his head with the buffalo skull on it out of the water and yelled, "Those who touch my body will have everlasting life!" So the sisters said, "Oh, let's go over there and touch him, and we will live forever." They came over and touched Spider, and Spider laughed to himself, "Ha! I'm right. I can fool people. I can tell them anything and they will believe me."

So then Spider hit his head against a tree and broke the buffalo skull open. He started walking again and he saw a family of great buffalo. He shouted to the buffalo, "Hey, brothers, I'm starving to death," as he ran his fingers across his ribs. "I'm hungry. I am dying." The buffalo replied, "Sorry, Spider, there's nothing we can do." Spider pleaded with them, "Please, make me one of you. You buffalo family are very powerful, and you have medicine." But the buffalo answered, "No, Spider, you're going to desecrate us. You're going to do things you're not supposed to do."

"Please, brothers," said Spider. So finally, the buffalo gave in. "OK Spider, you stand there," they said. "We're going to run and we're going to touch you, and you're going to become a buffalo." Spider stood there, but as the buffalo ran towards him to touch him, he jumped aside, and they missed him. He begged and cried again, so the buffalo gave him a second chance. And the second time they came at him, they touched him and he became a buffalo.

Spider was overjoyed! He started eating, rolling around and throwing dirt up in the air. The buffalo family started racing up the meadow and cried out, "Come on, Spider. You can come with us. You are our family now. We have made you part of our family." But Spider replied, "No, I want to stay here and graze. This is a beautiful place, and I'm enjoying every bit of it." So the buffalo family left him and went on.

As Spider grazed, he saw Coyote running over the hill. He yelled, "Hey, Coyote, come here, brother!" Coyote came over to Spider, who was a buffalo now, and Spider said, "Look at me. I'm beautiful - broad shoulders, small waist - I'm a beautiful-looking beast. Coyote, would you like to be a buffalo?" Coyote thought about this for a while, looked at Spider and told him, "No. Why would I want to be a buffalo?" And Spider replied, "Because you're going to look like me, and you and me can be buddies." So, as Coyote stood there, Spider jumped around with his tail in the air like a buffalo, circling and hopping around in all four directions, and he ran towards Coyote and touched him. But instead of Coyote turning into a buffalo, Spider turned back into a spider.

So what does this story teach you? It tells you that when the Great Spirit gives you something, you don't mess with it. Sometimes people are given a gift. Instead of keeping it to themselves so they can help people, they desecrate themselves by going out and giving it to somebody or by trying to analyze and understand it. By doing this, they end up having nothing. When something is given to you, you don't try to give it away. And you don't try to make people the way you are. That's what Indian psychology teaches you.

Some Iktomi stories taught me to respect all living things.

Squirrel Story - When I was young, I had a slingshot made of ash wood and an old inner tube. I was really proud of that slingshot, so I went out one day and shot a squirrel. My Grandpa Frank told me to take it to my grandma and ask her to cook it. So she made a soup with that squirrel and he told me to eat it. As I ate the squirrel, my grandpa said to me, "Why did you kill that squirrel? He didn't ask you to kill him. He is a creation of God. He was there to harvest food for his relatives. He was there to hoard the food so that, in cold weather, his relatives wouldn't starve. But you have taken his life. So, from this day on, you will live the life of that squirrel." And to this day, that is what I do. I hoard food and give it out to the people in the wintertime.

Robin Story - One day I took my slingshot and killed a robin. Sure enough, they asked me to dinner at my grandma's house and I ate that robin. So Grandpa Frank sat me down a second time and said, "The robin was sent by the Great Spirit to welcome all living things back to life. He sings to the trees. He sings to the four-leggeds and the winged in the spring, so that new life will begin and there will be rebirth of the young ones. Because you have killed the robin, from this day on you will sing to the people and Mother Earth."

Mangy Dog Story - When I was older, I had a single-shot .22 rifle and I shot a mangy dog. I felt so bad for this four-legged grandfather . He was itching, his skin was rough and he was really suffering, so I took his life. Grandpa Frank made me burn him. (Good thing he didn't tell me to eat him.) He said, "This dog was a reincarnated man. When a man does not have respect for any living thing, has no compassion for two-leggeds, four-leggeds or wingeds, has no compassion for his wife or his grandchildren, and takes the lives of others, that's what he comes back as - a mangy dog. And you will take the place of this mangy dog. You will suffer for the people. You will do things for the people and you will put your life on the line."

Other Iktomi stories teach you to be generous.

Fat Chief, Skinny Chief Story - The Great Spirit sent two warriors down to earth to be chiefs. He said to them, "My sons, you go down there and do what you must do. And when I call you home, come home to me and tell me what you have done." So these two warriors came down to earth. One of them became a fat chief who had a beautiful white tipi. He kept it so clean, it was just like snow. And he took care of his horses - they were clean, beautiful and well-fed. And his wife was happy and jolly. There was a wonderful relationship in the fat chief's home.

One evening, they sat down to eat. The wife brought out two big plates of food when, out of the bush, came a mother and her two children. So the fat chief said, "Hey, sister. Bring your children." He gave his plate of food to the mother and her children. He took the children aside and talked to them about the life they were going to go through - the hardships, the wonderful ways, how they must help their mother and father and set a wonderful example for them. He said wonderful things to these children. And when a grandmother came out of the bush, the fat chief called her over and said, "Mother, sit down. Here is a plate of food that we have saved for you." So the grandmother ate.

The other warrior became a skinny chief. His tipi was dirty, his hair was messy and his horse was skin and bones. All he did was lay around all day and scream at his wife. One day, he was preparing to be fed. One gigantic plate of food was brought out to him. When he got his plate of food, the skinny chief started eating. He didn't even share any of his food with his wife. Then, out of the bush came a mangy dog, starving and barely able to stand. The skinny chief looked at that dog - wagging his tail, humbling himself with his head down. He picked up a stick and beat the dog, and chased him away. Then he sat down and ate everything on his plate. He didn't leave anything for his wife and family.

And so, when it was time for them to leave the earth, the Great Spirit called the two warriors back home and asked them what they had done. He told them to look in the tipi of the skinny chief. There they saw the skinny chief's wife sitting all alone by his body. She had a smirk on her face, knowing that she would now be free. Nobody else came to pay their respects. Meanwhile, when the fat chief journeyed home to the spirit world, people came from all walks of life - grandfathers, grandmothers, children, young men carrying wild game on their shoulders. The grandmas and grandpas cried, "Who's going to take care of us now that he's gone? Who's going to feed us? Who's going to feed our children? Who's going to talk to our children? Take us instead, oh Great Spirit. Let him remain on this earth." Everybody was crying.

This story is yours from this day on. It teaches you that, if you want to learn this way of life, you have to give of yourself. When you pass someone on the street who's hungry, hold out your hand and feed him. Do your share like

I do. These stories that were given to me, I live by that rule. I once had a vision of the roving angel. In a dream, I saw a man standing in a mall, trying to shake hands with everyone. I came up to him and held out my hand, and he shook it. He smiled at me and said, "You are one of us." When I asked him, "One of what?" he replied, "A roving angel." When I woke up, I had a warm feeling in my heart, and it lasted for the next four months.

The spider stories, the coyote stories, the creation stories from east to west - these stories come to you like that as a child. They are part of our traditional way of life from the time we are born to the age of five, six or seven. I call them "Indian psychology". They tell you to be aware of things. They teach you to figure out the things that you're going to go through. And they teach you common sense - the difference between right and wrong. These stories are part of the holistic teachings of our elders. I was taught by my elders to learn with my eyes and learn with my ears. They said, "Look at the people. They are going to say things they are not supposed to say or do. They're going to do things they shouldn't do." You learn from these.

You can not counsel anyone in your life unless you have experienced all the hardships that they have experienced. This is the respectability of our elders. My teachers and others were very stern. They were strong-minded people. That is how I was trained. I was taught to do something on that pot or get off. My teachers were not there to serve me. I was there to serve them. I earned my keep. I kept quiet and I listened. I was not allowed to speak out. I was not allowed to ask questions. I was a soup-carrier. And I was honored if they invited me over to carry water to them, or drum.

By the time I was nine years old, I started to understand why the elders were planting their ways into me - the eagle staff, the grandfather, the water spirit. They taught me the sixteen doorways of healing - the spirit doorways. They taught me the mind spirit, the five - taste, hear, feel, see and smell. They taught me equality. They taught me not to point the finger. They taught me to feed the people - to fly a red flag at my house. (Last year during a meal after Sun Dance, there were one hundred and fifty-seven people eating. Food is the supreme law of our Indian nations.)

In 1954, I sat down with my grandfather, Frank Young Man Afraid of His Horses, on the east side of his log cabin. It was summertime. There was a beautiful moon coming over the horizon and he spoke:

"Grandson, understand that our white brothers have come here in turmoil looking for themselves because they have killed their leader. They need help. They are going to come here. They're going to tear up the mountains and dig holes to look for themselves. They're going to look in the water and under the water. And they're going to cut trees to find themselves because they do not know who they are.

"They have killed their teacher and, in turn, they are a lost tribe. One day, when I am gone from this world, back to the spirit world, you will find them up there. They're going to look for those things that God has given us to leave well alone. They're going to always want to know things. They're going to always take things without asking. No one can ever own this land, the water and the air. We are here a short time to give thanks to the Great Spirit. We must go from generation to generation and teach the love to our children - how we must hunt to survive, how we do not abuse, how we do not waste, how we only take what we need to live.

"Our white brothers will want you some day. They're going to want your ways because they have no ways of their own. One day, pity them. Teach them the ways that we live because they are not happy. They guide their lives with their God who they have created and they will try to buy you with their God - which is the frog skin, the dollar bill. Pity them. Pity the blacks they have brought here. Pity the yellow people they have brought here too. Because they will blame you and this country for everything that goes wrong, but they will never look at themselves. They will point their finger but they will never look at the three fingers that point back at them.

"The Sacred Pipe and the laws that the White Buffalo Calf Lady has brought to us are never to be broken. We must love and teach. The Great Spirit has told us that this tribe is going to become nothing, for they will disappear into the colors of the yellow, black and red. And in the end there will be one way. There will be one heart, one mind and one spirit. There will be love.

"Until that day, you must learn their ways and respect them as they will respect us. But understand that you are not one of them. They will never take you because they can not own that which they can not see - your spirit. Our spirit is powerful here in North America where we live. We are the winged and we are the four-legged. We are the fire, the water, the air and the earth.

"Grandson, go learn their ways. I will be long gone when you will help them find themselves. Teach them the right way. Teach them to give of themselves, not to take. Teach them how to cry so they will have feeling. Teach them to listen so they may understand. And teach them to be quiet so they may find themselves. You will live long enough to see something that no man has ever witnessed. I will be gone then. When the time comes, as she may return, you will see her. And the laws of this spiritual world may never be broken. They will be here. Each man has been given the right and each woman has been given the responsibility to live their life as they see their journey. Never take anyone's mind into your hands to make them like you, because we are all different.

"There are four lives that, as a man, you must live. You are created by two spirit persons - your mother, of whom you are the flesh and blood, and your father, from whom you inherit the fire. You are the warrior. You journey as a man from the time you come into this world. Your mother has loved you and your grandmother has loved you. They taught you to love your companion - to take care of her and to respect her. They taught you to love your children - to be with them and never leave them behind, because it is selfish to want to learn all things for yourself. Your children are most important. They must be the ones who understand. You must walk by example and attitude in the circle of life.

"When you are born, the second mother is there to wipe your mouth and kiss you and breathe loving air into your lungs. And you come into this world with love. Like the first great-grandfather - the spiritual man who was born in a manger - you are born on a bed of sage and straw. He was a star man. And we, the Indian people, are star people. That is why when you were born, my grandson, you had a star quilt to begin your journey.

"You are being given a name - Looks for Buffalo. And they cry with you because they know you will have a hard life. You will be ridiculed, you will be spit on, and they will make fun of you. They will call you a liar. You will go through the pain of learning but your spirit will never be broken, for you are given an eagle plume to wear as your namesake. You will be loved by your grandmother, your sister, your mother. You will be taught by your grandfathers, by your spiritual fathers - your uncles. Understand that as a man, you must go forward and never turn around. You pride yourself in what you believe.

"And the time will come when they will put paint on your face. All the people will come to see you and they will eat. They will celebrate you as a young man - that you have shown something in your life to earn the Red Hawk feather as a warrior - as a Kitfox, as a Tokala. You will journey upon this earth. You will always stand for the old people and the children for they are helpless. You will not hold a grudge against any man. You must always look back and know where you come from.

"You will go into battles. Some day, a lot of your brothers will join you to stand up for this country and a lot of them will not come back. But when you do that, you will enter your third generation, where you will be a warrior and you will receive the Eagle feather. For then you have become a man. And you will take a companion. You will fly like two eagles in the sky. And when the time comes that one of you must go home, the other must continue on what has been given - the right of life for people.

"You will stand up for your children and love them. You will feed them. You will set the example and attitude of this young generation. You will teach them. You will teach them to help people. You will teach them the sacred ways - the Sweat Lodge, the Sun Dance, the Vision Quest. You will ask for nothing in return, as what you have been given in life is enough.

"And in your final journey to the north as an elder - as your horse awaits you, as your time of death awaits you, and as your grandfathers and ancestors await you - you will gain your owl feather. You will gain the wisdom of the owl and your head will turn as white as the bald eagle. You will have the alertness of all wingeds and you will understand the power that the four-leggeds have let you use. And you will understand the spirit journey that you will make - the final journey completing the circle of life.

"Until then, you hold out your hand and give thanks every morning for a new day - in the spirit hour, which is 3:00 am. Give thanks for each day that passes, for you have made friends and you have made enemies, and tomorrow it will be gone. Feed your family, feed your friends, protect the young and the old. Never let anyone use your mind in the circle of life. Because, if you do, you will falter and you will fall. Never carry your companion. Walk beside her and respect her because she is the mother of your children. Never ask to help somebody - just go ahead and help. Never ask anyone if they are lost. He who asks anyone who is lost, they themselves are lost."

These messages are not from a man-made book. They have been passed down to me by my elders so that I may pass them on to others. I come from the Lakota tribe where we practice these ways to this day. The offering of the water, the offering of the air, the flesh and the heart - our elders left all these teachings for us to carry on.

If it is prophesied that you are going to be a spiritual leader or interpreter, you are treated as such when you are born. You do not touch the ground for one year. You wear beaded moccasins. For one year you eat nothing but venison, buffalo tongue, heart, lung. For one year, the grandmothers carry you. And when you go potty, they ceremoniously dig a hole in the ground and bury it. Because they know you're going to suffer throughout your life serving the people. They cry for you even as a young child because they know you are not going to have an easy life.

The grandmothers teach you from the age of nine years on up and you start thinking in a good way. They show you what herbal medicine to use for cancer, tumors, etc. We have medicines that speed up child birth. We have medicines for ladies who can never have children again. All these medicines are taught. Today, there are two hundred and forty-seven western medicines that have their roots in our Indian traditions. Pharmaceutical companies have liquefied and processed them, and they sell them over the counter.

At age twelve you go into manhood and you are taken into the circle. Everybody cries - your mama, your grandma - because now you are going to become a man. They paint you and they teach you how to stand up for the people. I thought that was all they were going to do to me, but here they also took parts of my flesh - in both hands. That was what they asked for. I didn't say no. As we enter the age of adolescence and become men, we go into ceremonies. We are tutored by our grandfathers by example and attitude - to never say "no" to anyone, but to put your family last and go. It is what you have taken as your vocation in life - that you will forever walk forward and never say anything bad to anyone.

In our culture, when a young man enters the second generation of life, he is given an eagle feather. And he is given his earth name, or spirit name. My spirit name is Pte Ole - "Looks for Buffalo". That simple name has a lot to do with what I do. I look for shelter for the homeless. I speak in places where I raise funds and ask for donations of food for the needy and the elders. I am always doing something because this is the vocation that each spiritual leader takes on. You walk with humility because that was given to you by your mother. You walk with quietness that comes from your mother. You walk with an obligation to help others. That comes from your mother. You walk with setting a good example, and that comes from your mother. You walk with thanks every day for everything that you have - "Wopila!" That comes from your mother. And then you walk with giving life for the future, and that comes from your mother.

I will always remember the words of my grandfather Frank Young Man Afraid of His Horses. "This is your mother," he said, pointing at the earth. "She gives you food. You must respect her. From the morning star to the evening star, to the north star, to the spirit doorway - where I stand, one day you will stand. And this is the only part of your life that you're going to give to her." What he meant by that was a grave. He told me that, when I was born, the only companionship I was to look forward to was death. And I must prepare for it. I must prepare my children and I must prepare my companion.

And so, my grandfather walked me through the adolescent age when I became a man. I believed then what I still believe today - that you have to go and serve your country - and I signed up for military service. I did it with pride because I felt that this country we were fighting for was ours. I believed that it would be benefited by our children, and their children, and their children. I took my grandfather's teachings with me overseas. I served with honor and respect. When I came home, I came home disabled, but yet I had pride.

When I returned from the service, I was welcomed back into the circle. All my grandfathers were watching me. Then, one day, my Grandpa Fools Crow stood in the middle of Kyle High School gymnasium and pointed out all the men who were sitting. All the spiritual leaders and elders there said "Me?" And he said, "No." "Me?" "No." Finally, they ran out of people to point at. I was the only one left. And so somebody pointed at me, and Fools Crow said, "Yes." I almost went into shock. "Why me?" I thought. "All these people from my home town, all these elders from here - why me?" Then I thought, "They might laugh at you. They might think you're a holy man." I couldn't believe I was chosen. I felt really insecure because here was a great man who people listened to in Washington D.C. "Here I am," I thought, "a guy singing in bars, crying at home, throwing up in bed, having blackouts, not remembering from one place to another, getting into fights. Why me?" But young men like me were being watched since early childhood.

Fools Crow stood before the people in Kyle and told them, "I will give this Sacred Pipe bag of mine to my grandson here." And he whispered to me, "All I ask you to do is stand up for the people and pray for them. But always remember that you're not a holy man. Always remember never to walk trying to imitate somebody else. You have your own journey to fulfill. Always remember to look back where you come from. Always remember to look down and feed the needy - the four-leggeds. And always remember to look up to our relatives who some day will come."

At the time, I didn't understand everything Grandpa Fools Crow told me, but I accepted it. So, I went to the Sun Dance and learned other things in that sacred circle: that the spiritual circle that we honor as Sun Dancers is a woman; that the altar we sit at is a woman. I didn't know any of this. I was an egotistical male. I had the European culture knocked into me and I really thought that we men were the boss. But I learned right away that the highest honor in that circle is the grandmother, our mother, our sister. I was taught this already, so that was easy.

I entered the Sun Dance circle and they sang the sacred songs as I danced for four days without food or water. And, sure enough, a voice inside me said, "You're going to fall down from that heat. It's going to hurt you." I listened, but I kept going. Then the voice said, "The people are going to laugh at you," and I almost backed off. But I looked around the Sun Dance arbor and saw the spirits of my ancestors on horseback - standing, watching - and I prayed again. I could see heat rising, and things got harder. I said, "Honored grandfather, pity me," and I danced for the grandfathers. Then somebody grabbed my wrist and led me around the circle, and it was OK. I was honored to do that, but again, my analytical mind hit. I looked around and I was afraid that my life was going end. Nine years before, my cousin went through this experience. He told me to always remember which hand the spirits took to honor me. Nine years ago they gave it to me in my left hand.

As a person who prays for the people, you must also sacrifice for the people. You have to do special things for them. You utilize all the wonderful things that you walk with in life - cansasa, kinnickinnick, red willow tobacco, the Canunpa - the Sacred Pipe, the cedar, the sage, the sweetgrass, the water and the fire. These are the sacred items of your altar. We spiritual interpreters listen to grievances but we can't always do everything. So, if I can't help someone with a certain sickness, I know that one of my spiritual fathers will, and I will send them there. One of my grandfathers was Jimmy Jackson, an Ojibway elder from Cass Lake, Ontario. He and I exchanged people. And I have a spiritual uncle from Saskatchewan - a great interpreter named Rufus Goodstriker. But, like Jimmy Jackson, a lot of these elders I work with are going home to the spirit world ahead of me.

All the spiritual interpreters and leaders on this island get along very well. It is the people around us who make up stories. It's the people around us who try to make us go against each other. We don't speak out against each other because we know that we are one blood and we know that we all carry that Sacred Pipe that the Great Spirit gave us to stand up for the nation. Wherever we see each other, we shake hands in greeting. And we talk spiritually. You might say that spiritual interpreters were the first to communicate via the Internet - the "Spiritual Internet."

We spiritual interpreters are not holy. We live a certain way. Believe it or not, we are often the subject of controversy - because people know we're not going to say anything bad. That is the way we live. We have been taught, "Why justify false accusations?" That's just the way it is. Forgive. Don't pay attention to it, because those people who are not important are going to bite at you. So it's better not to say anything. Those things come at you as a leader. You are taught to give your life. And the day you spill blood on that buffalo skull is the day you commit forever.

When I was a young man standing in line, I saw many of my uncles and grandfathers standing in front of me. Today, at the age of fifty-eight, as I go into the ceremonial grounds, I see only one man ahead of me - my spiritual father, James Dubray. I never stop to wonder whether or not I want to be in that position some day because my next trip will be the journey into the afterlife. I know that some day, that is going to be true. Sometimes I want to run. I feel like saying, "I'm tired. I want to sit down." But I go on.

It has taken me twenty-three years, traveling from the west coast to the north, to become a spiritual interpreter. Wherever there is a Sweat Lodge, I will journey through there. In 1992, I said my final prayers in the Gulf of Mexico. Now the spirits have allowed me to return home to my reservation in order to take over where my grandfathers have left off. My grandfather Fools Crow has given me his sacred bag to pray for the people. Wherever I walk, I walk with my "leksi". Today, my spiritual father and uncle James Dubray and I are protecting the original Sun Dance of North America. It has been handed down generation upon generation.

When I was young, my grandfather Frank Young Man Afraid of His Horses gave me a good lesson about respecting my elders. One day, I came by his house on my horse and he was digging a cellar. So I said, "Hey, Grandpa, you want some help?" But he didn't say anything and just kept right on working. After a while, he pointed at me and motioned me to sit down. So, I got off my horse and sat down with him, and he told me to bring him a clover stalk, so I did. Then he told me to bring six more, so I did. He said, "Grandson,

I'm going to tell you something today that you'll never forget." He told me to break one stalk, and I did. It was easy. Then he told me to put all six together and break them. I tried, but I couldn't break them.

And he said, "This day, my son, you have belittled me. I am a man who's been through life. I touched my first man on horseback when I was twelve in the last fight at Red Cloud Agency. You have belittled me today. The clover stalk that you have broken - that is you. The ones you could not break - they are me. Never belittle a man as long as you walk this earth by asking him if he needs help. You go and help, and do what you have to do. Never ask him if he needs help because every man on this earth has strength, and he has a spirit that must be respected."

Do not use your elder and do not make a mockery of him because he sits to the north and you, as an adolescent and teenager, sit to the south facing him. His teachings and his values are put into you to carry on your journey. Offer spirit food every morning, noon and night. Whenever you eat, you have a plate where you put your offering to the spirits. Say "Pilamaya" - thank you. Say a little prayer. Eat with your ancestors and good things will happen. These are the things I was taught.

Now I have a medicine wheel with two rows, two white eagle feathers, beads and a buffalo tail that hangs down. And I have a medicine blanket that's all beaded. My leggings are beaded and my moccasins are beaded. Just a few years ago, I was gifted with a tipi and I was given a bucket. When you're given a bucket, it means that you're going to feed your people. Getting a tipi means that you're going to lead the nations into one. When you're gifted with a buffalo skull, you are a chief, and you're going to sacrifice with that. The daughter of a chief gave me a staff with twenty-one eagle feathers, which means that I have attained everything I was to do in thirty-eight years. Last year I was presented a buffalo war bonnet. It means that now, I have a lot of responsibility. These gifts are not given to people to glorify them. These things are earned. I have earned everything that has been given to me over the years.

I have permission to talk about these things. I asked my elders if I could talk about them and they said, "Yes. The time has come. You must tell them how hard it is to go through the things you must go through in order to be where you are today - so that the chosen ones will take that road and those who play at it will listen." These teachings have come from a long way back - the respect, the dignity. But we are losing sight of these gifts that have been handed down. We want to minimize. We want to hurry up and get it done. When you have a great love for your teacher or your elder, you honor him. You take some tobacco out of the pouch, pray with it in the six directions, put it in red cloth, bundle it up and give it to him. It doesn't take that long - no more than five or ten minutes. Take some food to your elder. Give him a gift.

A lot of people want to find the spiritual way and live it but they do not want to give of themselves. This is where the desecration is happening. This is why a lot of our spiritual leaders are dying off - they have been used up prematurely. They should be around to this day. Our spiritual healers and interpreters are expected to travel from one place to another to heal and help people, yet they don't have a dime and they don't know how they're going to get there. We must have a giveaway. Too many people violate themselves by desecrating spiritual leaders or interpreters who ask for help. And so, the genuine interpreters - the ones who speak the spirit language - are getting scarce. Some of them elect to go on the other side of the path, called the dark side. There it is a lot easier to live because they can drink, they can smoke, they can make fun of people, they can criticize and they can judge. But the true spiritual path - the true spiritual self - takes patience, respect and enjoyment of life. Every interpreter comes through a road of hell. They become good-for-nothing alcoholics. And yet, these are the ones who are usually chosen by the Great Spirit to help the people.

These days, in our journey through the seven fires, the young people do not listen to their elders. I travel all over talking to young people who strike their mother or father, who strike their companions, who strike their kids. They do this because they are hurt. They do this because they are asking for help. Every one of us is beautiful. Every one of us is a spiritual token, here upon this earth for a short time.

Everyone in this world is a teacher. Some will teach you not to do the things that you are doing. Others will teach you by their example - whether it's good or bad. Our job here is to teach each other. If I teach you, I expect you to teach others. Don't keep it to yourself. Go out and love the world. Learn the rituals and the ways so that you can attain this level. Respect everyone. Never say anything bad to anyone. Give them the right to fall down and help them stand up. Wipe their tears and you too will have a happy life because they, in turn, will help you to fulfill your journey.

Never judge anyone. Do not judge the man on the street who is having a hard time because he may be the one. He may be the Great Spirit in disguise and you may miss your test to join the afterlife. The Great Spirit never created anything bad. The Great Spirit never created anything evil. The Great Spirit who I love and follow is loving and kind.

And so, I would like to say a prayer for our elders - all the grandmothers and grandfathers who have gone home from the face of the earth and left their knowledge and their heritage for us to carry:

Grandfather, bless our elders. They are the grass roots of our nation. They have earned the four sacred feathers that you have set forth for them - the plume of the tribe, the hawk feather, the eagle feather, and now, the owl feather. Grandfather, bless our elders so that, as they journey home, we may take their place. We are next in line and we look up to them for their knowledge and wisdom. But one day, that is going to stop and then we will have nobody to look up to. When they look around and look the way we come, they will see our children, and their children, and their children, and our grandchildren, and their grandchildren.

Chapter 4: The Rituals of Life

From the beginning of time, we have one goal in common. That is death. We all have a choice in life to decide which journey we are going to take. In our journey and destiny, we will meet with destination. And in that universe, we have symbols of the four-leggeds, the buffalo, the bull, the man, the lady, the medicine and the bear. All of these stars teach us that we are put upon this earth for a reason as Indian people.

We Indian people believe that the Great Spirit - the spiritual circle of the universe - is a woman. She has two daughters: the daughter of emotion, the moon; and the daughter of life, the sun. And she has a grandmother, Mother Earth, who gives us food. Here in North America, we believe that hers is the most important of all the families. Here, we believe that the power of this island is the woman. We are taught that the White Buffalo Calf Lady has brought the laws of this red island - that we are all relatives and that the sacred color of the Sacred Pipe is the color of our blood.

Here in North America, the men are taught that the woman is the supreme law. In our homes, our grandmas and our older sisters are the boss. And the Indian man knows his responsibilities. He prides himself in being the provider and protector for his family. He teaches by example and attitude but he only teaches when his mother tells him. In the house, his mother tells him to do this and do that and he listens. I may help a lot of people throughout the world but when I go home, my mother tells me what to do. And when I speak to the nation on the radio, I ask my uncle if it's the right thing to say. There are no laws or requirements to try to change anything. It's there. We are born with it. The man has to stand up for his family, provide for his family and teach his boys. The boys are the responsibility of the father. The girls are the responsibility of the mother. In your family, your female companion may sometimes try to advise the boys. But tell her, "No. That is not your territory. That is mine. Your territory is the girls. Talk to the girls. Prepare them for womanhood." This is the chain of command that we live by.

Every one of us is created for a reason. The Great Spirit has given us a circle of life. Our physical formulation has been created by the blood and flesh of our mothers and the energy force of our fathers. Every one of us has the blood from our mothers. This is where tender love comes in. From the time that we come forth from the east, we enter the world through the sacred canal with the water, which is the birth canal. And when our head touches Mother Earth, we start our journey to our final day of death. A midwife receives us and lovingly holds us as she cleans the mucus from our mouths and gently blows air into our lungs. Then she kisses us so that we begin our lives with love. This is the way we begin the sacred journey of our lives - the circle of life.

Because our energy force is not yet strong enough, we are breast-fed. Our mother's milk serves as a sort of antibiotic that keeps us healthy. During this time, our grandmothers and grandfathers receive us. They prepare a feast of welcome to honor our entry into this world and they honor us with our name - our true self - which comes from an ancestor, a dream or from the spirit world. When an elder is asked to give a name, he or she is first offered tobacco, then honored with a gift, like star blankets, a horse, etc. And we are given an eagle plume to represent the identity that we must carry while we walk here on this earth. From that day on, we journey. We begin the circle of life.

From the time she is young, the woman carries one half of the sacred four-directional cross called the Medicine Wheel. The man carries the other half of that cross. The woman carries a Sacred Pipe that is L-shaped. The man's is T-shaped. When you put them together, you formulate a cross. When you put the spiritual circle of life over the two Sacred Pipes, you formulate the Medicine Wheel. And when you put on the stem of the Sacred Pipe, you see the cross that women and men must bear while they are here on this earth.

The Ways of the Woman

A woman is the outer circle of this creation. She has six lives to give: learning as a child; giving life; caring for and loving her children and her companion as a mother; returning as an elder; and completion, which is death. The woman is the foundation of the family.

When a girl reaches the age of adolescence, her mother and her spiritual mothers braid her hair for the first time. And they anoint her forehead with the sacred color of mother earth, which we call sand paint. They part her hair and they paint her to signify that she has six lives to give in the circle of life. And she is given a ball made out of rawhide to throw. She must throw the ball as far and as high as she can so that she may live a long time. They say that if you don't throw the ball very far, then you don't expect to live very long on this earth.

And then she is given the teachings, the learning. When a woman starts her moontime period, she is taught that she is being purified by nature. At this time, she should be in harmony with the cycles of the Mother Earth and the cosmic forces of the universe. She is taught that she should isolate herself from men and society in general in order to purify her mind, body and spirit. It is a sacred time for a woman - a time to diminish herself in order to recreate herself. It is a time of contemplation, meditation, prayers and personal atonement. It is an opportunity to center herself and bond herself with the earth forces. She should approach her moontime in a spiritual and respectful manner with prayers to the moon.

Since nature is purifying the woman, she will be discharging contaminants, toxins and negative energy. At the same time, however, the cosmic forces of the universe will be replenishing her with power. It is for this reason that the young woman is taught to isolate herself and to stay away from certain foods, drugs, alcohol, sex and domestic and cultural duties. She needs to center herself in order to cultivate her power. She should not give away this power because it can be harmful to her and others.

The young woman is taught that moontime is a private and personal ceremony with herself and the earth. It is a mystical, magical and mysterious time that should not be looked upon with shame or considered punishment. The woman's moontime can help a woman fulfill herself. It can help her develop self-reliance and intuitive and psychic abilities, which are necessary for her survival. It is a time to cultivate her dreams, tap into her unconscious and synchronize her physical, mental and spiritual consciousness. The traditional Indian woman considers her moontime to be a mystical experience of enlightenment. Hence, she approaches the five-day ritual with respect and responsibility.

Indian Women's Moontime and Spiritual Laws

The following spiritual laws were given to traditional women to guide them during their moontime. They helped to protect them and others around them from sickness, disease and harm:

> **1.** *Avoid cooking, handling or eating the meat of any four-legged wild animal for the entire ten-day period, even though your discharge may last for only four, five or seven days.*
>
> **2.** *Abstain from drugs, sex and alcohol for the entire ten-day period.*

3. Do not swim in oceans, rivers, creeks or ponds (other than those specified as "moontime ponds") because such places are the home of the spirits.

4. Stay away from sacred mountains, deserts or valleys because such places are the home of powerful spirits.

5. Do not participate in religious dances, ceremonies, funerals or pot-lucks because others may be contaminated with your moontime power, toxins and negative energy.

6. Never touch or handle any religious regalia, bird feathers, or any physical part of a wild animal.

7. Do not gather or prepare sacred herbs and medicines during moontime, except for plants specified for moontime use, like clover tea, yarrow tea, etc. - moontime teas used as relaxants.

8. Eat green leafy and raw vegetables, drink lots of fruit juices, and eat foods high in protein such as fish, eggs, cheese, beans, etc.

9. Bathe in cold water instead of hot, for strength and purity.

And the young lady is taught the beautiful part of womanhood - motherhood - because she is the sacred circle of the universe. She is taught about the giving - that some day she may have a family, that she love and care for her children and her companion. In that circle of life, she and her companion will fly like two eagles in the sky. She prepares him to go into battle. And she sheds tears because, on this trip, he may not come back. This lady lives longer than the man. This is why the man is always served first. He is honored because he is going to die first. These two eagles fly forever, and when one of them goes home to the spirit world, the other eagle never mates again. It flies forever by itself.

Therefore the man always advises his children and his companion what to do if he leaves. He trains his companion to be the leader of the pack among his children and grandchildren, so that she is strong. You women whose husbands a lot older than you, remember that your man is going to go home earlier than you. Listen to him. Prepare your children. I prepare my children and I prepare my companion. We are born with the reality of death. We prepare to go home. We teach our companions what needs to be done.

The woman is taught to revere herself. She must never imitate a man. She must never speak down to any of her brothers or talk back to her father. She is taught to conduct ceremoniously all the responsibility within her family. She knows about herbs. She knows how to prepare the "wasna" - jerky made from pemmican. She feeds the spirits in the spring and in the fall, when the cherries are black. Three times a year she prepares the feast of the drum. She knows how to prepare the spirit food and she knows how to prepare the spiritual flags - the offerings - because every woman is the spiritual altar of creation on this earth. She is the spiritual circle. The man is the servant. The man is not the boss. It was a lady who brought the Sacred Pipe and also the drum. She is the drum-keeper and the medicine-keeper. And she is revered like the White Buffalo Calf Lady, or Guadeloupe. She is special.

Then the woman journeys towards the third generation of her life - eldership. And so, the lady, now a grandmother, begins to sew a blanket for her daughter. There is a dog that lays beside her as she works. When she stands up to tend the fire, the sacred four-legged gets up and unravels that design. So she sits down and tries to finish her daughter's blanket. They say that when a four-legged does that, your life gets uneasy on this earth. You lose respect for yourself. You are not attaining what you are supposed to do as a woman. You are a gift from the Great Spirit.

When the grandmother finishes sewing the blanket, it is time for her to go home. She has lived through a life of learning and giving - giving children, giving advice, caring for her children and loving her husband and family. As she gets elderly, she reaches the end of her journey and the completion of death. This lady is also given a sacred name. She is highly respected. She has her granddaughters. She is the total ruler of her clan - the family. She has been a child, she has been a young lady, and she has been a mother. All of this is what she owns. When she goes home, a feast is prepared in her honor and there is a big giveaway of a star quilt. Her Sacred Pipe is usually given to her granddaughter and the name that she carried on this earth is passed on to a granddaughter to represent her and carry on the sacred circle of life.

Spiritual Laws to Consider for Good Health

1. Be proud of yourself. Keep yourself clean and well groomed. Keep your heart, your mind and your house in order.

2. Respect yourself, your husband, your parents, your children and your elders.

3. Guard yourself against jealousy and hate from within yourself and from other people by using your aura.

4. Get up early every morning and offer prayers and song to the sun and earth. Pray for your family and the earth.

5. Pray to the plants and the herbs before you pick them. Apologize to the plant for taking its life.

6. Do not hunt or fish. Do not make men's weapons, regalia or other religious instruments such as drums.

7. Never take the life of a bug, plant, frog, snake, animal or bird needlessly. It is against the Creator's law to torture his creatures for experimental or wasteful purposes. Their life is sacred too!

8. Do not have sex upon sacred mountains, in the oceans or rivers or upon ceremonial or burial grounds if you want to stay healthy and well.

9. Do not pollute your mind, body or soul with drugs, alcohol or evil thoughts.

10. Learn and practice the laws, customs, religion, arts, philosophy and language of your culture.

11. Seek spiritual help from Mother Earth. Bond with her. Protect and preserve her.

12. If you are spiritual, you will have equality and never be inferior.

The Ways of the Man

The man has only four lives to give: learning as a child; giving as a man; returning as an elder; and completion. When a male child is born, the mother's head faces east. She is bedded down on sage and hay. The male child enters this world with his head pointing west. This direction signifies that he is beginning his journey of death.

The First-Born - If he is the first-born son, the grandmother elders prepare him for one year. He is given a beaded skull cap and he wears beaded moccasins with beaded soles. For one year, the first-born son is always carried, his feet never touching the ground. He is fed tallow, tongue and heart from buffalo or elk. And he is given a name by one of his grandfathers, who has a vision and responsibility for him. At the end of one year, people are welcomed from far and wide to view the baby. Now, he is in the teaching of his grandfathers and grandmothers, who take full control of his learning. He studies language, history, medicine and leadership. This teaching continues until he reaches the age of puberty.

Puberty - At the age of twelve, the young man's hair is tied in two braids. In the Making of the Spirit Journey, the young man eats the heart of a turtle. Now he begins his journey of learning to be a man. He is taught the respect of the sacred ways. He learns that we are born with twenty-one rituals or powers - seven come from the fire, seven come from the water and seven come from the earth. He is taught the respect of the physical powers that we utilize every day: taste, feel, see, hear and smell. Those are physical responsibilities that we have - our body, the physical form. And he is taught the sixteen rituals that he must go through to complete his own life. These rituals, added to the five, make twenty-one. Divided by three sevens, it makes up the holy trinity. And through this learning, the young man prepares to become a warrior.

Becoming a Warrior - This young man is taught that the warrior prepares himself for death from an early age. Everything that he will acquire in his life - the knowledge, the things that will be awarded by his own tribe, the bravery - he will prepare these gifts for his sons and daughters. When he becomes a warrior, the man has his face painted. To this day, we still practice that in our tribe. He is taught that, as a warrior, he must always stand up for the beginning and the end, for the young people and for the old people. He must give his life for his people. He has to earn the respect of the Great Spirit. He must go forward but never turn around. And he must be willing to give his life in honor of his people.

These ways have been handed down to this warrior. He has been given the responsibility of North America - the flesh that we are, the earth. He was given the responsibility to protect Mother Earth and to teach - to be the example in attitude for his children, with a lot of respect. This warrior is taught to give thanks every day. He is taught to help feed the poor. He becomes a great hunter. He is taught that he is one of the six chiefs. He is a hunter, he is a soldier, a Kitfox - protector of the people. He is also a camp chief. He makes sure that everybody camps right. He is a speaking chief - he talks to the people. And he is also a medicine chief which nowadays, we call a counselor. He talks to the people - those who have lost their loved ones. He wipes their tears and feeds them. And he is also a decision chief, which means that he has to make some very good decisions in his life.

The 16 Rituals of Life

1. *WATER - the first power we encounter when we enter this world through the birth canal. It is the blood that flows through our bodies and it is the water of Mother Earth - the rivers, lakes, etc.*

2. *AIR - the power that is breathed into our lungs when we are born. It sustains us throughout our lives.*

3. *FIRE - spirit force - our energy force. It is the heartbeat that keeps us alive.*

4. *EARTH - our flesh. The earth that we live on.*

5. *FOUR-LEGGEDS - they provide us with food, shelter, tools and weapons.*

6. *WINGEDS - grandmother eagle, the hawk and all other birds. They give us energy force used for doctoring and they help us find missing things.*

7. *ROOTS - provide medicines for doctoring, healing.*

8. *STONES - used in the Sweat Lodge ceremony for purification and healing.*

9. *THUNDER SPIRITS - they balance and harmonize the universe and the earth. We use these forces to doctor people.*

10. *RED WILLOW (Tobacco) - used in ceremony as an offering to the spirits when asking for healing.*

11. *TREES - cottonwood or maple for the Sun Dance ceremony, cherry for worship, cedar for healing.*

12. *SAGE - for anointment and blessing.*

13. *SWEETGRASS - used in the preparation of all spiritual ceremonies.*

14. *WIND - tornadoes, hurricanes, etc. - used to govern the climate of Mother Earth.*

15. *EARTH SPIRIT - snake, mole, praire dog - any spirit that lives underground. Helps in healing serious diseases.*

16. *KEEPING OF THE SPIRITS - pertains to death and the ability to communicate with the afterlife.*

Preparing with the Sacred Pipe - The man's responsibility is to prepare himself every day. He must get to know himself. When he makes the decision to carry the Sacred Pipe, he must go to a dreamer/pipemaker and offer him gifts. The pipemaker will dream the formulation of that Sacred Pipe and create it out of red stone. When the man receives his Sacred Pipe, he gives a feast for his friends to announce that he is preparing to know himself. He must always take care of the Sacred Pipe in a respectful way. He must find himself a good teacher, who will teach him peace, love and harmony. He will be taught the good ways of discipline. He will be taught all the ceremonies - the name-giving ceremony, the burial ceremony. He will learn about the power of the fire as a firekeeper. And he will be taught how to prepare the Sacred Lodge - the womb of our mother that purifies us - and how to conduct a lodge ceremony. He will be given a name and the spiritual clan that he must walk with - the winged clan, the four-legged clan. And he must honor himself with that Sacred Pipe. He must not drink or use any kind of drugs. (It was a lot easier to live in the old days because things were only one way. Nowadays, we are a multicultural society with many different ways, and it is a little harder.)

As he prepares himself with the Sacred Pipe, the man begins to understand that he must learn from others. From others he will see things that he is not supposed to do and he will hear things that he is not supposed to say. He must not judge any man. And he must remember that, just because he carries the Sacred Pipe, does not mean that he is holy. (I have been told that there are no holy men on this earth, only gifted men. They are called spiritual interpreters.) As he journeys forth and walks with time, the man prepares himself every day in the spirit hour of 3:00 a.m. (A lot of people ask me why I wake up at 3 o'clock in the morning. It is because your spirit is calling. If you have an uneasy spirit, you might be doing something that is out of line and the spirit is telling you that you must do something about it). And each day, this man gives thanks to the day. He gives thanks to the Great Spirit and Mother Earth. He gives thanks to the four-leggeds who give him food to eat, so that he may feed his family. And he gives thanks to the spiritual winged ("guardian angels" in modern terminology) for guiding him.

The man is guided every day. He must not worry about yesterday because, in his journey on this spiritual path, he is born a red man, he is going to walk a red man, and he is going to die a red man. He lives one day at a time. And as he journeys forth, he walks with respect for the gifts that God gives him. He has kind words for his fellow man and for families. Now, he is the father, the grandfather and the uncle that children do not have. Now, he plays one of the major roles in his life - to be there when the children and the elders need him. And he must give the finest things to the needy people in his journey of life - the circle of life.

Inipi - The Sweat Lodge - The man must purify himself in the "Inipi" or Sweat Lodge. The Inipi lodge is made of sixteen willow poles bent to meet each other, crossing in the center. They represent the sixteen doorways that we must cross in our circle of life. In front of the lodge there is an altar made up of a mound with a stake in it, signifying the sacred medicine tree that we use on this earth. The top of the stake is Y-shaped, signifying that the man has a choice of two roads. He can take the short one or the long one. When the man attends the Inipi ceremony, he conducts himself in a quiet, modest and respectful manner. He refrains from loud or rude behavior. He doesn't walk between the altar and the lodge or the altar and the fire pit. And he must never spit into the sacred fire or stand around it and talk about others. The only one who is allowed near that sacred fire is the firekeeper, who prepares the stone family - the grandfather rocks.

When he goes into the lodge, the man is entering the womb of his mother. And so he humbles himself by crawling in, just as he crawled before he learned how to walk. As he enters, he greets his ancestors with the words "Mitakuye Oyasin" - "All My Relations". From then on, he must not talk. When he and his brothers are seated inside, the seven grandfather rocks are brought in, representing the seven laws that were given to the people by the White Buffalo Calf Lady. One by one, the grandfathers are anointed with herbal medicine to honor them. Then the water is brought in, the door is closed and he begins to pray. Once the prayers begin, the spirits enter the Inipi and the door stays closed so as not to break the ceremony.

The man prays for understanding and respect. He prays never to say anything bad to anyone. He prays that he may humble himself and walk quietly. And he prays for the people - that he may reach out and hold the hands of the children and the elders. The spirits will recognize him and they will work through him. Wherever he goes, people who are hurt will come, and he will touch their hands to let them know he cares. And finally, he prays for help with things that are bothering him. He leaves his problems with the grandfathers and Mother Earth, having faith that they will be taken care of. When the ceremony ends, the man crawls out of the Inipi and again says "Mitakuye Oyasin" as he passes through the door.

In the old days, men and women did not sweat together. But today, with so few spiritual leaders around to lead Inipi ceremonies, mixed sweats have become common and acceptable. I believe that there is nothing wrong with this, so long as the person conducting the Inipi does it in a strict and respectful manner. The Inipi leader must know the spiritual meaning behind the ritual - the sixteen doorways, the grandfathers. He or she must first teach the participants how to prepare for the Inipi. Then, during the ceremony, everything that is going on has to be explained to them. These are big responsibilities, not to be taken lightly.

Hanbleceya - Invision - One day, when he is strong with the Sacred Pipe of knowledge, the man prepares himself for the thirteen eagle feathers - the thirteen moons, or thirteen months, which represent one year - guided by his spiritual leader or teacher. This teacher has chosen his vocation from early childhood. We call him a Medicine Man today. He talks to the spirits and the spirits help him to help people. As a spiritual interpreter, he works from one world to the other. The man learns for four years. In each of those four years, he purifies himself in the Inipi for "Hanbleceya". Some people today call it "Vision Quest", but I prefer to call it "Invision". In the last month of preparation, he must not contaminate his body by having sex.

When he is ready, the young man ventures into the wilderness on one of three mountains located in the center of North America. One is Devil's Tower, which we call "Bear Butte". The other two mountains, also known as Bear Butte, are "Sun Dance Butte" and "Thunder Butte". They form a triangle. And there is another triangle of spiritual powers located on this earth - to the north, in Canada. It runs from Sioux Lookout down to the Canada/U.S. border. Another triangle is located to the south - in New Mexico, Arizona and Colorado. In the east, from New York City into Canada and to the west, there is another. Each of these triangles is 360 miles in circumference. They have been located here and given to the natives of this island. They are the sacred doorways of our journey.

In one of these places, the young man will get to know himself. He goes to this place to Invision - to look at himself and what he has gone through in his life. There he will be put inside an altar and "locked up". The sixteen doorways will be opened up and he will be left there to pray for as many days as he can. He will not eat or drink anything. He is not allowed to speak, lay down, sit on a soft blanket or go out of the altar. There he will talk to the Great Spirit and to himself, and learn who he is. He will look at himself from early childhood and see the things that bother him and hurt him the most. He will make an inventory of himself to understand and prepare himself. Though he has lost his father, or his father didn't raise him, or his mother didn't raise him, he is grateful because his mother and father have brought him into this world. He is grateful that he has been given life. He must not blame his parents. They have done their share of responsibility bringing him into this world.

We prepare ourselves for this Invision - the hurt that we have come through since early childhood, the things that happened to us. And then we ask to understand. We, the Indian people walk in our destiny. There are no failures and there are no mistakes. The things that we look at negatively are actually something good for us to learn. So the next time you are confronted by those things that hurt you in the past, you have the chance to go around them and not be hurt. You must never let anyone use your mind to hurt you. You must walk with forgiveness. And when you climb that mountain, you work with yourself to understand love. Love begins by respecting yourself. You can not respect anyone unless you respect yourself. You can not forgive anyone unless you forgive yourself. You can not help anyone unless you help yourself. You can not feed anyone unless you feed yourself. You can not cry for others unless you learn how to cry to understand the way of life.

You go on that mountain to give of yourself. You give the only part of yourself that you own on this earth - your flesh. That flesh is God-given. This is what you give back to God when you kneel down. This is what Jesus was trying to teach the people - to fast on the mountain, to find a direction. Jesus was a great spiritual leader. He was a red man - a Hebrew. He went to Hanbleceya and learned from the wilderness. He went to the wise men to learn his herbal medicine. He left his family when he was fifteen and came back when he was thirty years old. He had learned a lot in fifteen years. He went out to help people and to heal the sick because he had faith and belief. All of these beliefs are still here on this earth. We the traditional people still carry them. In all of our tribes - no matter what our language or denomination - any way we pray, the Great Spirit hears us.

The Sun Dance - When he has prayed on the mountain for four years, the man has finished one year of learning. (In the old ways, four years of learning were equivalent to sixteen years.) And, when he so desires, the man enters the Sun Dance. There the young warrior is painted and, for four days and four nights, he must dance in the hot sun without eating or drinking anything. And so, the man prays for four days, and at the end of those four days he purifies by piercing himself.

Through his teaching, my grandfather Frank Young Man Afraid of His Horses explained the meaning of the Sun Dance. He taught me that the supreme law of the universe was the woman and the circle. One day he pointed at the moon and said to me, "You see that? That is your grandma. She guides her daughters with emotions. There's two sides to that. During that circle of time, the lady folks honor themselves to suffer for us. They spill blood. And the sun, the life-giver, is your mother also. She gives life to us. Under that sun, the man spills blood for the woman." When he told me that, I understood what the Sun Dance is all about. And I understood why my mother and my sisters went through the cycle of moontime.

The woman is the giver of life. She gave life to a man called Jesus. She had a sister, who was the sun. This is why the Sun Dance happens. It is a re-enactment of the sacrifice of the first medicine man, who we know as Jesus. He shed blood for us from a staff. From a staff like that hangs an eagle feather representing every deed the man has earned, or a fallen warrior - every person. This is why he hangs an abalone shell, a medicine wheel, an eagle feather and a red cloth from a staff - to symbolize that he has shed his blood upon this earth for his mother. In the circle of life, the power that I speak of is all based upon the woman. The woman is the supreme altar. With the Sun Dance, the Invision and all the offerings, the man is the only one who sacrifices himself. For that is his road. That is his own offering. The four-leggeds utilize the power. The wolves and all those you pray with will accept you. They will come around. They will put their spirit inside of you. They will be your namesake.

There is a way for everything - from the time of the Inipi to the preparation for Hanbleceya to the preparation for death. The elders have always taught us that we have come from beyond the Milky Way. The Milky Way is a symbol of the direction of life - good and evil, evil and good. And the Milky Way has an altar here on this earth. It is called the Sun Dance Tree - the tree of life. It is the only tree in this world that is identical to the human body. Where I come from, this tree is the cottonwood. In Canada, it is the maple. And from that tree of life come the five spiritual medicines: the willow of life - "kinnickinnick" - the blood of our nation; the sage; the sweetgrass; the cedar, which we burn to purify ourselves and drink to purify our blood; and the cherry tree, for worship during Sun Dance. There is a long history of healing behind these medicines. When we go on the mountain, we learn the value and importance of these medicines for our people.

Nowadays, people go to Hanbleceya and say they're going to fast for four days. They're using their analytical mind. Then they go for two days and they feel guilty for the rest of their lives because they have not achieved what they said. But I was taught that we don't set days or times. We just say we'll pray for as long as we can. The same thing goes for the Inipi and the Sun Dance. And these days, some people go and Sun Dance just to say they did it. They come out and they drink alcohol, and they brag about their piercing marks. This is not the way it should be. Desecration is setting in this Red Road of learning. It is important that people prepare themselves wholeheartedly for the rituals of the Inipi, Hanbleceya and the Sun Dance. Some people say that they have Sun Danced for four years, so they are finished. But when you follow this way, the spiritual circle is forever. You are never finished. That is why I encourage people to think twice about going on this Red Road.

Every year, young men and young women from all over North America come here for Sun Dance. Some of them are surprised to learn that, during those seven days here, you can't sleep together and you've got to get up every morning at 4:00 am. When they find this out, they turn around and go right back home. At Sun Dance, you sleep for three or four hours a night and do everything early in the morning. You dance from 4:30 am until 9:30 at night. One of the highest honors we've seen here in recent years came from Vern Harper, a Cree elder from Toronto. He was the oldest Sun Dancer there. That brother went four days and four nights without food or water and danced all day. He inspired the younger Sun Dancers to keep going.

This is not endurance. This is how you attain your chain of thought - your heart, mind and spirit - how you prepare yourself for one year to go into that circle. It's very important. If you're going to tutor yourself to prepare for that circle, then learn how to get up at 3:00 am every morning - 365 days a year. If you don't make it, start over. My home is always open during Sun Dance ceremonies. But if you come here, you're no guest. You have to do the grunt work. Everybody works together. But the children learn best because they learn from the grass roots. Wherever I travel, I invite the young men to come to Sun Dance - to learn, to help and to see if they can carry water for four days. And I invite the ladies to come sit and honor the men who are suffering, so that life can go on. I tell them to learn before they come. I say to them, "Learn the songs. If you're going to pray on the mountain, learn at least two or three songs. If you're going to the Sun Dance, learn what it's all about. Don't go there cold turkey."

Eldership - And as he gets older, the warrior earns respect. Like the bald eagle, his hair turns white. He has gained the wisdom of life because he has seen many hard times and he has seen many good times. He becomes a dreamer - a medicine dreamer. He becomes an arbitrator - he settles arguments. He becomes a good counselor among the people. He is a wise man. He becomes a medicine chief, because he knows the herbs to help the people with. The final part of our journey in the circle of life, eldership, is the most beautiful. It is a time when we must earn the owl feather, the fourth feather in our journey of life. The grandfather owl has been superstitiously branded as a bad omen, but in fact, he is a grandfather who gives us messages - both good and bad news. In many tribes we respect that grandfather because he teaches us to prepare for our eldership. When we receive the owl feather in eldership, we prepare to go home.

Going Home - Death - When it is time for the man to journey home, a caretaker is appointed. The caretaker prepares him between the north and the west. He places an eagle staff at the head of the man's resting place, the coffin. He ties the six sacred colors to stakes and places them in buckets filled with earth around him. There is a buffalo robe and a buffalo skull facing south, representing the man who is going home. And they prepare the "Gray Horse", or "Medicine Horse". (People have different versions of the journey. I only talk about the Lakota ways.) The Gray Horse is tied with the finest feathers to his tail and mane and, when the time comes, the great warriors of the past (in my tribe Crazy Horse, Sitting Bull, Red Cloud, Rain In The Face, Kills White Buffalo, Kills Crow, Young Man Afraid of His Horses, Spotted Tail) bring him to you.

And when you die, you are dressed in the finest - all the things you have earned in your life, like your eagle feather. You have your eagle staff which you have attained in your life. You have done many deeds. You have attained twenty-one eagle feathers that you have set to accomplish in life. You have a chief's headdress. You have a buffalo tail with a medicine wheel with two feathers. You have your beaded medicine blanket. You have your Sun Dance whistle. And when you are laid to rest, beneath you there is a buffalo skull laying upon a buffalo hide. All these spiritual gifts that the Great Spirit has given you are prepared for you.

On the first day that you are laid to rest, you are prepared for your journey. You are wiped down with medicine and they put paint on your face. Sage and cedar are laid on your resting place. And all the things that you have earned in your lifetime - like your eagle feathers - are on display. A tipi is erected in your honor and "wasna" (pemmican made into jerky) is prepared for your journey. All this is done by your sisters. They prepare you and pray for you, as in the time that you came into this world from the east - through the birth canal, with the blessing of the water. On the second night the Red Hawk feather is placed in the south, representing your adolescence - the time when you were given war paint on your face, your Red Hawk feather, and the destiny of worship from your grandfather.

On the third day, they place your eagle feather in the east, representing the identity that you have walked with on this earth. You earned this when you became a man and took on the responsibility of the family - to stand up and provide for your family and your children. Your sisters cut their hair, wrap it up and give it to you for your journey, so that they may stay in contact with you in the spirit world. On the fourth day, at 3 o'clock in the morning, they sing songs for your journey home - your naming song, your warrior song, your Tokala (Kitfox) song, your family song and your final journey song, honoring your achievement of the owl feather. You have fulfilled your journey of life. And the finest of food is prepared for you on your journey.

On the fifth day of your journey home, the winged are called in. Every flying creature that has guided your life and blessed you in your journey is honored - your eagle feathers, your eagle fan - all of them are prepared and blessed. And on the sixth day, they prepare the horses that you have. Any four-legged that you have is respected and honored. Throughout those six days, they sing for you every day and they feed the spirits on your spirit journey.

On the seventh day, you make your final journey. All your warriors carry you and escort you with songs to the final resting place that you have chosen, your eagle staff ahead of you and the buffalo skull behind. There, you are laid to rest underground. (In the old days, you would have laid on a scaffold above the ground.) Sacred medicine stakes are planted at the four directions of your grave. From the four sacred stakes fly the four sacred colors: black, the color of the thunder people; red, the color of the white buffalo four-legged power; yellow, the color of the beginning of life - the star people who we come from; and white, the color of our spiritual journey. These four sacred colors - as well as the green and the blue, representing Mother Earth and the universe - are tied to the stakes. At the head of the stakes is your staff, adorned with your eagle feathers and your eagle whistle.

And the rest of your belongings - everything you own - are put in your tipi, and the tipi is burned. If you so desire, your finest horse is killed at that time. From that day on, your companion and children must walk in your place, keeping your memory alive here on this earth. They feed you every day with spirit food. And the family continues on as if you are still living among them. Your sons and your grandsons become part of you, because you have taught them well. Your daughters and your granddaughters are part of you, because you have taught them to respect themselves as women and the givers of life. And your companion never remarries. She walks the rest of her life to honor you, until the day comes when she too journeys home.

And so, on behalf of the brothers who Sun Dance and all the grandmothers and grandfathers who have gone home from the face of the earth and left their knowledge and their heritage for us to carry, I would like to give you this Sun Dance song. This is a song of thanks to the Great Spirit for what he has given us. As we look up in the sky to the circle which is our mother, we give thanks for the things our mother has given us that are beautiful in our lives - the children, the woman, the husband, the family, the mother, the grandfather - everything that is created. This song says all of that. It says "thank you".

Tunkasila Wakantanka - Grandfather, oh Great Spirit
Eya Ho'e Wa'yelo - This is the way I throw my voice at you
Canunpa Wakanca - the Sacred Pipe is holy
Ma Ya K'u Ca - you have given it to me
Pilamaya Yelo - thank you very much

Chapter 5: The Seven Laws

When the White Buffalo Calf Lady came to the Lakota people, there were seven ceremonies in her bundle. During that time, the supreme law of the universe was the trinity: the daughter of light - the sun; the daughter of emotions - the moon; and the daughter Mother Earth. The Lady also gave us the Sun Dance ceremony. We were to use it to heal ourselves. In later years, we put the colors of the four nationalities in each direction - the fire, water, earth and air.

The seven laws were put here in North America for the Indian people. Just as the Europeans have the Ten Commandments, we the Lakota have seven laws, or virtues. All of our ceremonies are bound by these laws:

*1. **Walk quietly**.* Have a great mind - have patience, tolerance and self-control. This is why Indian people take their time getting to places and take their time to do things when it's time to do them. People sometimes call it "Indian Time". But we only have one life to give in the circle of life. We are born with the reality of death and we try to prolong death as much as we can. That's why we do things slowly and sincerely. You will see people violate this virtue. You see them going from point A to point B at one hundred miles per hour. They're always going fast, never realizing what's around them. My grandfather Red Cloud talked about many toads flattened out on the black road. He was talking about death on the highway due to alcoholism and careless driving. Through alcoholism, drinking and abuse of these vehicles, we will die.

We must treat our great minds with patience and self-control. Do not be in a hurry to get to the spirit world. You'll get there when your time comes. Until that time, prolong your learning. Take your time and you will learn beautiful things. Learn slowly, and you will remember. If you learn from books, you're going to keep looking for more books as you finish each one. It's not there. It's where the people live. That's where it's at.

*2. **Help others as you help yourself**.* Be generous. Give. In the spiritual way of the Sun Dance, we make a commitment here on this earth to do things so that we carry the needs of our people in our hearts. We are to be generous. We are to share and to give. The first virtue has always been violated here because the new generation we call the European North Americans are taught to take, not to give thanks. They are used to taking anything in their path. They should learn how to give.

Back in 1975, the Religious Freedom Act was introduced in the United States, and I was one of very few Indian men who stood up for the white people here. I said they had the right to learn this holistic way of life - respecting Mother Earth, the air, the water. I was damned and condemned for that by my own people. What I didn't realize then was that they were going to keep it to themselves. I never realized then that they were not giving people. But my grandfather Frank Young Man Afraid of His Horses taught me that we are equal - that we are one mind, one heart and one spirit. He taught me to teach my white brother to learn how to give of himself. He taught me to share my food with him. He taught me to bring him into my home. He taught me to talk about the creation. And he taught me to love him because he is one of us. He said it is up to us to bring him back to the circle and teach him right.

One day, I was driving through Minneapolis with my son. There stood a man with a little girl beside him. He had a sign that said, "Will work for food for my children." All the people driving by in their shiny cars wouldn't even look at them. My son said, "Have you got any money, dad?" So I looked in my wallet and found $28.00. I parked the car and my son went over and gave them our money. He came back to the car and we drove off. I asked my son, "What did that man say to you when you gave him the money?" And he said, "He called me an angel." I remembered the dream I had, so I turned around and went back to that block where they were standing, and there was nobody there. My son asked me, "Dad, why is it that they can't help their own kind?" And I said, "Because they're lost, and we have to re-teach them. We have to teach them to hold out their hand."

It is our children who teach us these compassionate ways. When was the last time you gave of yourself to something that was worthy? When was the last time you went to the old age home and sat with the mothers? When was the last time you made them feel good by giving them a Christmas present? I teach all over the country but, come Christmas time, I raise money for turkeys. I have friends who ship them down and give them out to the women. We don't brag about it. It's just the way we are. Our children know how to give. I'm pretty sure that when I'm gone, they'll be doing this. And their children will do it too.

Ask yourself, "Why am I here on this earth for such a short time?" The beauty of these gifts are yours. Practice them. Don't take them home and put them on a shelf. What is going to be left for the children? If we sell our

Medicine Wheel, if we sell our sweetgrass, if we sell our sage, if we sell our Sun Dance, if we sell our Invision, if we sell our Sweat Lodge - what is going to be left for them? Think. The money we make is good. My grandfather told me to take one quarter off from every dollar that I earn. Set those quarters aside and collect them, and then buy some food for the old people, the children. If you see a child with no tennis shoes or anything, go help him. If you see a young man with no jacket, go buy him one.

3. Love people as you would love yourself. Nowadays, in all the schools throughout the world, children are not being taught the tender loving care they should be treated with to learn their destiny. It's hard to understand for parents nowadays who have never been taught by their grandparents where they came from. They have only been taught that they must instantaneously take and claim everything in their path without compassion and love. But everything has a purpose, whether it is a four-legged, a winged, a two-legged, or a serpent. Everything has a legend and a life behind it. Every tree on this earth is a female and a male. The creation of the Great Spirit is a 360-degree circle. Everything that man has made is square, diagonal and even. They don't want to uneven themselves. Yet everything that God has created is perfect.

4. Respect others as you respect yourself. Have pity and compassion for all things that move - every living thing. This too has been violated. We're killing the very relatives that we have - the coyotes, the wolves. Anything that's supposed to be here in North America to balance and harmonize us, we're taking it away. We don't have pity. We don't have compassion for each other, for our neighbors.

We must have fortitude. We must have principles and live by them. When you take the sacredness of any object in your hand, try to understand why you're picking it up. Are you picking it up for show and tell or are you picking it up for real? Are you going to put your life on the line for what you believe in? I have scars all over my face because I fought for what I believe in. It was for the future. It was for the future generations. We were trying to bring understanding that we are the first family in North America.

Back in 1975, there was a situation in Canada involving the Anishnawbe. I rushed there and stood up for them. I taught them how to demonstrate on a road. We had a lot of fun. And just recently, when they were annihilating the buffalo in Yellowstone Park, one of my sisters who we appointed as leader went over there to speak out. And my brother Arvol Looking Horse was there too. This is the kind of people we are.

5. Set an example for your children. Children nowadays have no respect for their elders and no respect for their mothers. And the children are being blamed for that. It is not so. It is the mother, the father, the grandmother and the grandfather - they are to pass on this teaching - the respect. They need to teach their children to pray with spirit food at mealtime. They need to teach their children to smudge their house every day. They need to teach their children to offer water and food when a visitor comes. And they will have respect and honor themselves every day. This is how you bring back the circle.

Know your responsibilities. The supreme law of the house is the woman - the mother, the grandmother, the daughter. The man's authority is to protect, to feed and give good teachings. The mother tells the family what to do; the father is responsible for the teaching of the children. They must not be harsh. This too was lost because nowadays, parents are dictating to their children - hollering at them. Never once do they hug them, kiss them or tell them that it's OK if they have fallen and hurt themselves. These are the ways I was raised, so it bothers me nowadays when parents are mean to their children. I'm harsh with my children sometimes. It hurts me for days upon days because I have violated myself - the things that I was to carry on. Nowadays I am standing against a square world and its values. It is hard because I must be brave and courageous yet, at the same time, I must keep these things that have been handed down.

Walk with humility. We must seek to humble ourselves at all times. We must always humble ourselves in front of our elders and people who are older than us. This way we seek humility every day, with respect. It is the attitude and example you set with humility in front of your children that they're going to become with compassion and love.

6. Hold out your hand and bring everybody together. There's no more handshakes, there's no more compassion - only when there is something there to take, and then you do it.

7. Say thank you for your life. Every day when we get up, we must give thanks to the Great Spirit and all the stars. We offer prayers so that the Great Spirit may in turn give them to the needy, the poor and the sick.

Look at me how I walk, and listen. I'm a healer, but I gave too much of myself. And none of the people who I helped said "thank you." And now, I have to carry the burden. None of them said "thank you" to the Great Spirit - not to me. They all promised they were going to feed the people, take care of the children and care for the old people when they got well. But when they got well, they said, "Auf Weidersehen." People don't know how to say "thank you" anymore. It tells you in the Bible, "Kill the fatted cow and feed the people, for my son has come back to life." That's "thank you". It says so right in the Bible. Don't be like Abel and Cain, trying to have your brother murdered. These ways are real, these holistic Indian ways. Learn how to say "thank you."

Through all this learning we gain the wisdom and an understanding of the spiritual laws - the seven virtues. And we try to live by them every moment of our lives. These seven virtues are only the first set of laws. But there is a second set of laws that people never talk about, that we must always keep in mind:

1. The Water - The power of the water is the first law that we encounter when we come into this world through the birth canal. It is the blood that flows through our bodies and it is the waters of Mother Earth. It is the purity of the water - the holiness of coming into this world - that we must respect.

2. The Air - The second law that we encounter is the power of the air that we breathe. We must respect this air. When we are born, a midwife clears our mouths, lovingly kisses us and puts the power of the air into our lungs, and loves us. Nowadays, most of you probably don't understand why you are angry. That's because, when you were born in the hospital, the doctor grabbed you by the ankles and beat the hell out of your bottom. So you came into this world mad. That love is gone.

3. The Fire - The third law you encounter is the power of the fire - our energy force. Indians call it "spirit force". The Great Spirit gave us a fire. At the time when our destiny meets with our destination, this fire is put out and returned back to him. Because we have neglected the power of the fire, we now have physical complications in our everyday lives.

4. The Earth - When we are born, our heads are the first part of us to be anointed by the earth. The law of Mother Earth - our flesh - is the fourth law that we must respect. Today, the garbage that we throw away, the pollution that we create - these things we all violate together because we have lost respect, humility and compassion. We see junk laying around the road, yet we do not stop to give time to pray and lay it aside. It bothers me because I too violate those things. I get very lazy from this present-day life, not fulfilling my journey. We are desecrating Mother Earth. We are cutting too many of her hairs - the trees.

5. The Four-Legged - Have you ever heard of people who do "shape-shifting"? We use the power of the four-legged and see through their eyes to look in on people. Yet today, we have lost this respect and are needlessly killing many animals who live on this earth.

6. The Winged - Owls, eagles, bats - we look through the eyes of the winged to help us find missing things. Some people call this "psychic ability". Back in 1975, a plane carrying a bush pilot and two nurses went down near Thunder Bay, Ontario. They brought me up from the United States to find that missing plane. The spirits told me to sleep and showed me where it was. They showed me a lake in the upper right hand corner of a map. I didn't know what direction that was, so when I came out of that sleep, I went downstairs and looked at a map and saw "Dog Lake", north-west of Thunder Bay. There, in the north-west corner I saw a bright object and made a line to it. I asked how many miles it was from that point to Dog Lake, and I was told "30 miles". So I used that visual I got in my dreams from the winged spirits to see it. We found that plane. Everybody gave me credit, but it wasn't me. It was the spirits.

7. The Spirit Journey - This is the law of the after-life, when our destiny meets up with our destination. In order to prepare ourselves for our spirit journey, we must attain ourselves to a level of purity of heart, mind and spirit by going "Invision". Not to be confused with "Vision Quest", where you go out to look for something, Invision means asking yourself, "What have I done for my shortcomings of yesterday or this morning? How can I in turn change myself for the rest of the day?" But we have violated this too. We keep things bottled up inside of us - yesterday's hurt. We will never be able to bring these things back upon this earth, from the past to the present time. It is not worth it.

When you learn these disciplines and work with them, you can see the other life. This is why spiritual interpreters are not afraid to go home. When I get tired, I think about death's doorway. "Boy, I'm going to go home now," I say to myself. But I realize that I've got to look back. I have children, I have a companion, and I'm going to consider staying. If I leave now, I'm taking the chicken way out. It's not my time to finish. The seventh law is also the power of the Thunder Spirits, who balance and harmonize the universe and the earth. Their way is counter-clockwise. When they accept you, they take your spirit.

One day, the Thunder Spirits took my spirit. I was standing out in the Sun Dance grounds praying and, for some reason, I was thinking about the day I was going to die. And the Thunder Spirits answered me. They jumped out and came to my tipi and flipped it over. Then they went to the front door of the lodge, jumped over the pine tree arbor and hit me in the head. When they hit me in the head, I felt like I was physically there but I was withdrawn. It was like I was passing out. I heard beautiful birds, saw the trees, and smelled all the beautiful aroma. Such a beautiful place, and yet I still heard that Sun Dance song. Then the sound of the drum went high-pitched, like somebody put a steel bucket over my head and hit it with a baseball bat. Suddenly, I was coming back. I realized that I was back in my body. I was still standing there dancing, but everyone had backed away from me. Later I was told that I went off the ground like a rocket, blue flames coming out of my feet and hands. The Thunder Spirits took me on a trip and I lived. Now I have the right to talk to the spirits. I pray and the clouds go.

This second set of laws teaches us that, if we violate what has been given to us by the Great Spirit of the universe, we will suffer the consequences and bring back the harm that was brought to our first generation of life. (Our first generation of life was 500,000 years ago.) We have violated the first set of seven laws of respect and we have broken all of them in the second seven laws. Therefore we're bringing all kinds of hardship on ourselves: floods, earthquakes, fires, heat, famine, child neglect and family abuse. We blame the government and we blame humanity. But we must look within our hearts. We must listen to the words of the first spiritual man called Jesus - a red man from the Hebrew tribe - who told us that we must keep these laws and not break them because, if we do, we will bring water upon ourselves. And now, here we are, and we're blaming one another.

And there is a third set of seven laws that is never talked about because of the competition and the separation of the mind in our society today. It is in Buddhism - a very powerful sect in Asia. The very power they use - Domino, Ringo, Kao (past, present, future) - embodies the seven laws of the trinity. They have violated their first law of respect to all things. And so, they are suffering today as a result of their own technology. And the second law is the contamination of the mind - we call this the "666" - the separation of mind through competition, materialism, disrespect, physical and emotional abuse, the loss of family virtues, incest.

And the third law - materialism - is guided by the supreme law of money and finances. Yet, if you handle this the right way, it can be helpful. You can become a roving angel with this third law. If you set aside one quarter out of every four quarters that you receive, you will have the chance to redeem yourself with this quarter saved to give to the needy and the poor. And when that money leaves your hands, you have no concern about it because it doesn't belong to you any more. And this makes you look at your need to control everything around you.

The fourth law teaches us that we must strive every day to attain ourselves to the challenges of daily life, as this day may be our last day on this earth. You must always clear your mind to allow in the spirit. You must understand that the universe has a purpose. You understand the earth and you understand that we have relatives in the universe, who are also seven nations. Through Christianity people have become assimilated into a standard of worship of one day out of a whole week. Therefore, they're closed-minded. They're not open to the holistic way of life that we are to attain in our everyday lives.

This fifth dimension is the law of our relatives in the universe. It is law of the Avatars - the star people, and the law of the "Wakinyan" - the Thunder Spirits. We have known for hundreds of years as Indian people that our relatives would some day come back here and help us reorganize our earth. That time has come now. The fifth law teaches us that there is going to be great suffering until the 21st day of the 21st year of the 21st century. There's going to be much death on this earth. This is something that we must consider because it will not affect our children and grandchildren. They will have a better life when that time comes. But those of us who have diminished this chance for our young generation are going to pay for it. We have taken all we can and built all we can. Now we are answering. A wise man does not build his house alongside of a hill. A wise man does not build his house in a meadow. Only a foolish one will do so because he has no guidance of tomorrow. And in turn, he will suffer. What goes around comes around.

The sixth law that we must consider is the power of the wind - the hurricane and the tornado. The wind family is making us answer at this time by cleansing Mother Earth, so that good things may happen and grow in place. The law of the wind has come about because of our violation of the earth. Through selfishness we have dug up mountains and imbalanced this earth. Through greed we're also taking a lot of the hairs of Mother Earth

- the trees. We're imbalancing Mother Earth and speeding up her rotation. It takes seventy-five years to grow a full adult tree that will give us oxygen. But we are reversing this by trying to get the little trees to give us enough oxygen. These baby trees are like our children. They don't have enough energy to give. Yet we are not listening to this. We are developing technology that we think is going to control the world around us. We have gone as far as we can into the universe to study its laws and have come back here to attain them and leave them on this earth. But it is not working because we have lost peace, love and harmony.

The seventh is the law of self-destruction. It is the Seventh Fire that was prophesied. It was written about in the Bible, in the Book of Revelations. It is time that we are in now. We may have all the money we want for material things in our lives but we cannot buy the knowledge, the virtue and the respect that we need to survive. You can own everything you want to own but it's not yours because you're not going to be alive two hundred years from now. The people who take, take, take, and never give will never get to the other side because they have taken enough of this earth to remain here. There's nothing wrong with the belief of Christianity, but it has confused us long enough. The spirit has said that he is going to close down Christianity throughout the world - through fire (which is war), disagreement and politics. Churches will burn. This has become a reality.

These laws were given to us to violate so that we can become one mind, one heart, one spirit and one nation. We can't bring them back and turn our way of concern into reality. We must look to our grass roots - where we come from. By facing this reality, we will be able to understand ourselves and better our lives. People need to go back to their boundaries and know their history - their extended family. Where did I come from? How far back does my blood go? To the Vikings? To the Huns? This is very important to North Americans of European, Asian and African origins. This book is trying to tell them that they do have principles themselves.

The sacred circle that is in the universe is in the image of the altar here in North America. This goes back to the beginning, when the Lady presented the Sacred Pipe to the Indian people. Beyond that, most people do not understand the meaning of this because, at the present time, we are seeing assimilation and genocide in action. People today are becoming sick and unbalanced. They are committing suicide because of their confusion of life. People, through no fault of their own, have nowhere to reach for help because of the racism that is coming back to us before the turn of the century.

Here in North America today, we have a situation of racial authority versus spiritual authority. The supreme law that was created by man here is the government. This government is granting racial authority of control by the European culture. This is not to put down the government and European culture, but it means to understand that they're not of this land. Therefore, they have no spiritual authority here in North America. Spiritual authority here on this island comes through fasting and prayer - just like the first red man on this earth. His name was Jesus. He set these things for us to follow - the Invision, the purity of mind, body and spirit, the ceremonies he left behind, and the personal relationship with each other - not to judge or point the finger at one another, but to listen.

This is a buffalo island. The buffalo is the foundation of North America. If you look up at the stars in the universe, you will see this buffalo there - he is supreme. And here you also see the Grandmother Bald Eagle - the eagle nation. In the history of North America, the eagle from the sky flew in and took a beautiful princess from the tribe and mated with her. This is how the Lakota people came into being. The buffalo and the eagle - they're in the stars. And we are to guide our supreme altar - our recognition of these things that are in the sky. Nowadays, people use these stars to guide them if they're lost.

We the Lakota people are one with the buffalo. If we don't teach others to take care of the buffalo here in North America, when the buffalo are gone, we will be gone too. Because the supreme law of this island is the buffalo. The other animals that were brought to this island - pigs, chickens and cattle - have brought disease here. And now the buffalo are being blamed for these diseases. This is why we, the Indian people, need to look at our history. We have assimilated ourselves with technology. We are using all these superficial means to stay healthy but it's not working. Here in North America, we are the buffalo people.

The supreme law of this island is the Lady. The Creator gave us the law of the universe - the responsibility of women for bringing life into this world. And this law pertains to the way we have to live every day. According to our traditional ways, the woman is the foundation of the creation of the family, which is the tipi, and the foundation of the medicine roots, which is the plants. And we men must work with her to create a home and a life of respect, security and harmony for our families. Because the most sacred of all things is the woman, the man treats his companion, his mother, his grandmother, his daughter, his sister, his granddaughter and all of his female relatives in a sacred manner, with dignity and respect. Never was it our way to harm women physically or mentally. Indian men were never abusers. And so today, as men, we must always refrain from any kind of physical or emotional abuse. If we have these feelings, we will have to go to the Creator for guidance.

The things that we are talking about here come from the other side of the world because we, the Indian people - the buffalo people - live every day in communication with Mother Earth. Through the White Buffalo Calf Lady it has been prophesied that, in our way of life, we must pray every day for unity. Three white buffalo calves have been born in our life today: "Miracle" in Janesville, Wisconsin; "Medicine Wheel" in Pine Ridge, South Dakota; and "White Cloud" in Michigan, North Dakota. This is a prophecy fulfilled, for we have been told that, when the White Buffalo Calf Lady comes again, there will be a return to our old ways by the seventh generation, which is the turn of the century. So we as Indian people should not harbor any hard feelings towards any other spiritual teachings. Instead, we must teach respect and listening to our brothers and their families and their children because our blood is red as any of those who are created by God. Our devotion should be sincere.

The seven laws teach us that respect is the glue that will hold the people of this world together. It is a respect for all races, all species of life, and especially the woman, because a woman brought the Sacred Pipe to the Lakota people. The teachings that came with this Sacred Pipe are designed to produce balance and harmony among the people. Without balance and harmony, there can be no peace. Without peace, there can be no unity.

Chapter 6: The Twenty-One Powers

Back in the third century A.D., the ancient Hebrews introduced the western nations to the spiritual teachings of the "Kabbala". "Kabbala", meaning "tradition of knowledge", taught that there is an invisible law or force governing the universe - the tree of life - connecting everyone and everything. All is aware of all and nothing is left to chance. According to the Kabbala, the key to these connections is understanding numbers and the way they relate to each other. But as western nations formed, these ancient teachings were lost. The power of this spiritual knowledge was hidden, adapted and altered by priests, kings and leaders to suit their own selfish purposes.

Like the ancient Kabbala teachings of the west, the Indian people of North America have long believed that the Great Spirit gives each and every one of us twenty-one powers that we are born with. There are five that we are totally responsible for: taste, hear, see, feel and smell. These physical powers are governed by the "head spirit" that we call the brain. We use them every day. Then there are the sixteen spiritual powers that we have. We use these powers to understand our lives before we go home.

The Natural Powers

1. The Water - The power of life - the blood in our bodies, the rivers and lakes of Mother Earth.

2. The Air - The sustainer of life - the air that we breathe.

3. The Fire - Our energy force. The heart that gives us happiness, peace, love and harmony.

4. The Earth - Our flesh and Mother Earth, which is not to be desecrated.

5. The Four-Legged - The Sacred Buffalo represents all the four-leggeds of North America. If his numbers are diminished, then the people of this island will perish.

6. The Winged - The female Bald Eagle - the supreme law of North America - representing all the other winged of Mother Earth. Her desecration brings changes to the earth.

7. Wopila - Saying "thank you" at the time of death in appreciation for your journey through life.

The Supernatural Powers

8. The Thunder Spirit - The power of thunder and lightning. Horses are Thunder Spirits. Respect them.

9. The Water Spirit - The fish, the turtle, the loon - anything that lives in the water.

10. The Stone - Pipestone (Catlinite), the grandfather rocks in the Sweat Lodge.

11. The Roots - Sage, sweetgrass, cherry tree, cedar, and other medicine roots.

12. The Water Spirits - Rain, hail, floods and other natural disasters.

13. The Earth Spirits - Moles, snakes, lizards, groundhogs - things that live underground.

14. The Wind - The power of the tornado, the hurricane, the cyclone, the blizzard.

15. The Tree of Life - The cottonwood, the cedar, the maple, the red willow.

16. The Symbols in the Universe - The buffalo, the bear, the ram, the panther, the Milky Way, the Sun Dance Tree, the Pleiades (Seven Sisters), woman and man.

The key to these sixteen powers is discipline. Discipline is the law that you teach yourself to utilize. The key to that discipline is the Sacred Pipe made of a red stone that you can only find in North America. And the key to the power of discipline is just like a combination lock - thirty-three to your right, nine to your left, etc. Those are prayer sequences. The seven rituals that I have already talked about are a part of these powers. (Every tribe has a different version. I only speak about the ways of the Lakota people.) These spiritual laws are learned from our ancestors. They should not be minimized, played with or desecrated in any way.

The sixteen powers are governed by the spiritual doorways of the triangles in the image of the moon, the sun and the earth. Triangles - the Holy Trinity, the Kabbalas. This triangle formulation is also on this earth on four different islands - the islands of the black, red, yellow and white people. On each of their islands there are triangles joining three mountains. Here in North America, the island of the red people, a triangle joins three mountains - Devil's Tower, Bear Butte and Thunder Butte. Inside this triangle is a 360-degree circle. Every one of these triangles - the image of the moon, the sun and the earth - has a 360-degree circle in it.

The Head Spirit - Just as there are triangles in the universe and on the four islands of this earth, our bodies are also made up of triangles, or Kabbalas. The first triangle is from the top of our heads to our shoulders. When we control our lives from here, we don't do a very good job. This is the negative Kabbala - the square world that we have created for ourselves - the square world that controls us. Because the four nations - black, red, yellow and white - have chosen to guide their lives with the head spirit, each of them has violated the covenant that they were given to protect. The yellow people of Asia have violated the covenant of the blood, which is the water that flows in the rivers and oceans of Mother Earth. The white people of Europe have violated the covenant of the air that we breathe. The black people of Africa have violated the covenant of the fire - our energy force, the heart. And the fourth nation, the Indian people of North America, have violated their covenant, which is the earth - our flesh. Each nation shares these first four of the sixteen powers - the blood, the water, the heart and the flesh. By violating these powers, they have deteriorated their triangles or Kabbalas.

The story goes that, when the nations of this earth created the tall buildings to overthrow the Great Spirit, he demolished us by separating us by language, culture and geography (four islands). When we're going to try to overthrow the Great Spirit, we're going to come back together and try to do it with the help of the "666". What is that? Everything you buy has it - computer markings - the mark of the beast. How many of you know that? In the holy book it says that, when man appoints himself God, he shall create his own image. It's happening now. What do you think cloning is all about? And it also says that when man appoints himself as the ruler of this earth that he shall try to overthrow, he will use the mark of the beast. What is that? Computers. They have stunted our growth and our knowledge of reality. They have stunted our progress of thinking. Therefore, we don't even have faith in ourselves to put two and two together and come up with four. Because if we do that, we won't believe in ourselves, and we pick up the adding machine. That's how far we have deteriorated our minds.

The old traditional way of this island was based upon thirteen moons and twenty-eight days per moon. But since the new generation of five hundred years ago enacted its own calendar, it became an even number - twelve - representing the "666". Any even number represents the 666. And there was a star that was given to us by the star people, who we call our grandfathers. This star was made up of two triangles, like the "Star of David". It represented good and evil, evil and good, and we were to use it to guide our lives from each morning star to the evening star. But this also was changed - to the five-pointed star. Every one of the five-pointed stars that you see in the American flag is controlled by the states of the union. If you turn this star upside down, you will see the goat that represents the 666 - how each state is governed by the square world that man has been controlled by. But here in North America, man is not the controller. It is the woman, because she too has a purpose here. This is why all her children are coming here to reunite and try to save this world. And this is why we are going back to the thirteen-month, twenty eight-day cycle of our ancestors.

How many of you are alcoholics? How many of you like to get angry, throw things around and pout? How many of you think you have your life in control? That's the first negative Kabbala. The things that you have experienced for so long - the things that you have lacked all your life - make friends with them today. These are the most precious gifts - the negativity. We can use negativity to help others who are suffering - with alcoholism, adultery. These things are real. And if we make friends with them, we'll be OK because the Great Spirit has given us the spiritual circle.

Thinking with The Heart Spirit - The second and third triangles represent the six doorways - the power of the six directions. The second triangle goes from our shoulders to our breastbone. From here, we're going to think from our heart spirit with compassion and love. As young children we had no control over what happened to us in the place where we are born. Our mothers and fathers have done their duty - to bring life into this world, to set an example and attitude for our children. But that was really neglected by this square world causing a captive mentality, dependent on the system. Take two wolves from the wilderness and put them into a cage. These wolves will breed and have cubs. The caretaker will hand-feed them, look after them and clean out their waste. The wolf cubs will lose it. If the wolf parents escape and leave the cubs behind, the cubs won't want to leave.

This is the captive mentality we have created for ourselves with this square world. And now, we're going back to that. We have depleted the energy force of this earth. We have speeded up the earth now, and we're blaming the weather. Never once have we looked in the mirror and said, "We are the cause of our self-destruction." It's a lot easier to point the finger than to look at the three fingers pointing back at ourselves. All for the sake of a dollar we are destroying this earth. And at the same time, we're destroying our own physical journey - because we were born in that captive mentality.

We all live on reservations - in apartment buildings - co-dependent on our jobs. We have neglected all our other energy forces called the sixteen doorways. Why do you think we have Alzheimer's disease? Because we have not re-energized all those other points of energy force - the survival instinct, psychic ability. In our tribe we still practice that because we live on three million acres of land away from the outside world. Shape-shifting - taking the form of other beings, or astro-travel - looking into places and helping people - we still practice those old ancient ways that we are going back to. But what is holding us back is our captive mentality.

Alcohol, people say is OK according to Christianity. To us holistic people, it's only an escape. Alcohol makes you look old. I'm fifty-seven, and I know a lot of forty year-olds who look older than me because of self-destruction. Self destruction is in your mind. When you're angry, you look for an escape. Let it go. You're beautiful. If you're in a bad mood, call me and I'll cheer you up. We all go through that masochistic behavior. It's caused by ourselves and our ill feelings.

There's no respect in the family any more. There's no T.L.C. Mother and Father both have to work. Who knows what they do to our children in daycare. We have child abuse, sodomy. As we journey through life, a lot of us have been contaminated through sexual, physical and emotional abuse. Sometimes it comes from within the family. This is what I call that darkened road. We live with that hurt. Now the women and the men have come to the point of not trusting each other. The man who had the love of his grandmother, mother, sister, daughter, is always skeptical about women. He's afraid to let a woman love him. And the lady also goes through that. She's afraid to love a man because she has been molested some time in her life. This is a secret that we all keep in that darkened windowpane, thinking that nobody will ever know.

All this does is eat away at us. We'll never be happy. We'll always be blaming our companions. Some of us cry inside because we never had that love when we were growing up. We never had our mother and father there. We never had that T.L.C. when dad would hug you and say, "It's all right, daughter" or "It's all right, son." We never had that motherly love. And we men who had a dominating mother who told us what to do and neglected us, we're going to look for that mother the rest of our lives. Couples come to me for help because they're fighting like cats and dogs and can't get along with each other. I tell them to get away from each other and live happily ever after. And they blame me for trying to split them up. But you'd be surprised how strong their relationship becomes after that. They're back together and they're strong. What I use is called reverse psychology. I'm not here to try and save your marriage. That's your business. If you don't get along, get it over with. Get away from each other.

Cleaning House - And so we come to the third triangle or Kabbala - from your breast bone to your hips - cleaning house. Get a pencil and paper and write down all the good things you've done. Then write down all the negative things that people have done to you. Read it because you're going to find yourself pointing that finger. When you get to that, study both sides of yourself carefully... "I don't know who I am. I don't know where I'm going..." Deal with that. Look at it, because it's a good experimental cause. Don't look at yourself as a failure. The Great Spirit put you through those experiences to help others. Have you ever passed out and thrown up all over yourself? This is the kind of thing we don't want to admit because we don't want to be labeled.

If a man screams and hollers at his companion and she screams and hollers at him, the children are going to grow up the same. I come from a dysfunctional family. My mother and father had it hard. They argued all the time and eventually divorced. But I was very fortunate to have grandparents look after me because I was the first-born. If I didn't have them, I would have been out there. Now these things that we go through in life, understand that they're only temporary. Put yourself up on the hill for four days and find out who you are. But train yourself and prepare yourself for one year.

Happiness is in us. We create happiness. Take a walk with your kids. It will make them feel happy. Talk to them. Treat people how you want to be treated and that's how you will be treated. Don't be arrogant. Don't expect people to come and shake hands with you. That's what I do. That's my job - to make you happy.

Giving, Sharing - Learn how to give thanks. The fourth triangle, from our hips to our knees, is another negative Kabbala that we are practicing now - we don't know how to give. We know how to take. Giving means you give everything. If you see a homeless person on the street, don't throw him a quarter. Give him twenty dollars. The negativity that you are born with - recognize it and deal with it. The Great Spirit has given us these powers to share with one another and love one another. He gave us these sacred ways to save Mother Earth. Do not lie to yourself. Be willing to take that step. Get a good teacher. I had good teachers - Plenty Wolf, High Bear, Young Man Afraid of His Horses, Grandpa Charlie Red Cloud, Fools Crow. What they did is put themselves into me. So what you are reading here is their teachings. Take these teachings with you and give them to the next ones.

Working with The Spirits - The fifth triangle - from your knees to your toes - lets you work with the spirits. The spirits can help you. They can direct your life, protect you and keep you safe on your journey. People call it "mind over matter" when you pick up a red-hot stone or walk on hot coals without getting burned. These are the connections of the fire, water and earth - the three basic ingredients and the most powerful tools in this whole world. Anyone can be an interpreter of Mother Earth. We all have twenty-one powers that we are born with. It's the grunt work and dedication that we put into it that opens up the sixth Kabbala triangle, located in the middle of our foreheads, and makes us aware of these powers. It's the grunt work that develops our psychic ability - our healing ability.

First you must purify your mind and your body. Go in the Sweat Lodge and go into the wilderness for Invision. Do your meditation in the right season - usually the last part of May, and June. That's when all the spiritual ceremonies happen. Always wait until the first thunder comes. Before the first thunder comes, you harvest the kinnickinnick - red willow - to make your tobacco. Offer tobacco and pray, and scrape the bark on the south side. Cover the wound with sweetgrass and the bark will grow back. The cherry tree is the best spiritual medicine that we use. You also do the same thing to that. Take your shavings from the south side of the tree. Medicine men have spiritual journeys. They come from the cherry tree.

All of us have lost a loved one. Those of us who have hard feelings for someone who has gone home, pray for them every day. They're in a better place than we are now. This is our journey in our circle of life - to go through the life of learning, giving, returning and completion. The destination we are all headed for is the afterlife. Let's not be afraid of death and these changes that are happening, because every day we are going home. Every day, you get up and prepare for death. This is the reality that we come from. Prepare yourself.

Memory is the best medicine that we have. Never forget things. Don't forget to feed the spirits every time you eat. Put out a little food on the plate. In return, you'll be surprised. They will contact you - in your dreams or movements around the house. Love is the doorway to the afterlife. Always remember that when you deal with spirits. Learn the spiritual songs. In order to speak the language that the spirits understand, you need to learn the spirit language, which is the Lakota language. The power of the voice is so strong. If you train it to sing the medicine songs, the spirits will hear you and they will come. Singers use that song. There's a song for every living thing on the face of this earth.

I deal with spirits. I'm a spirit man. Some people call us psychics. We misinterpret that as "medicine men". A spiritual interpreter is someone who can interpret the unknown to this reality. You can diagnose people's bodies without X-rays. I have helped doctors all over the world. Some people call me when they don't know what's really happening. That's because they conduct their lives through machinery, from the outside only. I conduct my life by working from the inside out. Anybody can learn this, but if you start calling yourself a "shaman", you're going to stunt your growth. The human mind is very tricky. That is what's going to stop you. That is what's going to slow down your learning.

We live in an instantaneous world today. We want everything instantly, but that's not going to work. It takes four years to learn one year. By the time you finish sixteen years, you see miracles happening around you and you want more. But it's actually the connections you learn - the Kabbalas, the triangles, the sixteen doorways. All of us are born with these things - every one of us. Only some of us want to take the chance and try. This is why young men start with the fire. They make relatives with that fire and learn to understand its power. And after that, they graduate to Invision and the Sun Dance. Then they make relatives with the water and the food of the earth, because they're going to learn to get those from the air. They're going to drink the air and they're going to eat the air.

Understand the one hundred and one powers of each direction. There are six directions - the West, the North, the East, the South, above (Great Spirit) and below (Mother Earth) - each with one hundred and one powers. That's why it takes four years to learn something. By the time I finished sixteen years of learning from my grandpa, I only began. I've been at it since 1948 and I'm still learning. I'm learning to close my mind because I have an analytical mind. I've seen the dead wake up. I've seen people who have never walked, walk. It's not that you are holy. You're working with their energy force called the Kabbala doorways - same as yours - to get them going.

When the spirits honor you and work with you, then you can help people. You grandmothers are at the highest peak of force. If you have a grandchild who's sick, go to them. Wash their little feet with sage. Wash your hands. Sit down with them. Put your left hand on their feet and cradle them and you'll find out that your force is so much more powerful than their sickness. You can always help them. If there's someone with 104° fever, instead of putting ice packs on them, put your left hand on their head. On the back of our head there's a hole. The more you learn this holistic way, the bigger and deeper that hole becomes. Your left hand is your power source. All of us have that. Be very careful with your left hand because it is a healing hand. And your feet are very holy. Some of you who pray with people with hands-on - be very careful because you could get their sickness or disease. Watch your feet. Put some medicine in your shoes or your socks, like sage - whatever you have - to ground yourself.

If you want to work with herbal medicines, be prepared because you're going to live an isolated life for about two years. You're going to learn from the roots. You're going to learn how to identify them and you're going to learn how to find them from year to year, because they don't grow in the same place every year. And you're going to learn cures from the grandmothers. Be sure to keep some of these cures to yourself because somebody's going to get a hold of them and make money off of them. Today we have AIDS medicine that we use to keep people alive. Some scientists investigated me about this medicine and I said to them, "Yes, we can give you the ingredients, and you will probably find out what chemicals are in them. But I'll tell you one thing, the medicine will not work for you. Why? Because you don't know how to pray." When you use the roots, you've got to pray. With everything you use and everything you do, you pray. That is the way you train your life.

The stone family, the grandfather in the lodge - the grandfather that flies. The stone family is very powerful. You can learn how to use stones. You can heal with every stone. How many of you work with crystals? Crystals are purifiers. Be very careful when you use them to heal. You may create the wrong doorway. Align yourself with everything before you mess with them. You can clean people but you can also clean their disease into your own body.

But at the same time, you can use these powers - your psychic ability - to practice your own self. Lay flat on the bed with your palms up. Dust yourself from your toes to your midsection - the fifth and fourth Kabbala triangles. Collect all the dust to that point. Focus on the water source of the universe as a circle - a lake. Connect yourself with that and you can see through that. Once you start working, you're going to start seeing the stars first, seeing outside the bedroom and into the universe. Once you start feeling the coldness from your head and your feet and you've got a little force of hot energy flowing, you're preparing. Focus on your friends or the place where you were raised - that's the sacred part of training yourself. Do not focus any place where you've never been before.

Once you leave your body and see those places, you're learning. Don't stay out too long. Learn how to re-enter your body because if you stay away too long, your body functions will slow down, your blood pressure will drop, and you may not have enough energy to come back into your body. This is astro travel - astro healing. We do that. If somebody is sick over there, we ask them to make prayer ties as a sign. We travel from here to there to doctor them, then we come back. This is nothing to play with.

Thirteen is a number that is most sacred because it represents the trinity - the trinity of positives, the trinity of negatives, and the full moon. Some people say that thirteen is a scary number, but it is not. It is a sacred number. How you apply it is what it becomes. How many of you "space cadets" pray during the full moon? You're trying to get in touch with the after-life, but this is the most dangerous time to do it. Remember, one day after the full moon is the time to get in contact with the Avatars. Avatars are star people like us. They too have the powers that they gave us. The reason why I use the term "space cadets" is that we always want to reach the beyond to see what is up there. We forget to practice the doorways from earth first.

The power of the enemy - you can make the enemy strong. You can make that enemy control you. You can let that enemy destroy you. Don't let anyone use your mind. If you give them the power of your mind, they're going to control you. People use negative psychology to control. But if you love that enemy, he has no power. That is called forgiving. We find it hard to forgive. It takes a lot of struggle and prayer to overcome that. An eye for an eye - don't think revenge when you're practicing spirituality. Because the dark side may hear you and honor you but, in return, he will take one of your loved ones. Why justify false accusations? Forgive those who trespass against us.

I never teach people to follow me. I teach people to follow their own journey - their own destiny. Because you and I are different. You have your own destiny to fulfill. You have the same gift from the Creator as I have - you have the right to fall. I've only been there ahead of you so I can help you grow.

But some interpreters or so-called medicine men teach people to follow them around. And when they die, the people go back to drinking and fighting with their families.

Respect the passing of energy. Don't give your pure energy away to a "spiritual vampire". Spiritual vampires use kindness to suck your power. They always hang around you to listen to what you say and see what you're doing. They always want to know what's going on, what's going to happen. They don't have the gumption to find out for themselves and have the patience to walk. A lot of these spiritual vampires come to see me. They say, "Heal me, Floyd." So I pray for them, and when they're healed they go right back to their church and pray. They say, "Oh, I don't like that Indian religion." All of a sudden, they get sick again and they come back to me again. "Please heal me, I'm hurting here, I'm hurting there..." One day I got fed up with one of them and I said, "Go back to your priest and let him heal you, because as soon as I heal you you're going to go back there and make fun of me ."

You see, it's people who are undecided in their lives who separate how they walk. To me, I'm a Catholic, Protestant, Episcopalian, Buddhist - all of that into one. Wherever I have a chance, I get my holy communion. Wherever I pray, I pray in a church. Wherever I go, whatever tribe I visit, I sit down with the people and pray with them. That is how you must live in order to work with the spiritual power. As long as you do different things and get self-centered, the dark side is going to nab you. He's going to entertain you with some very good powers but they're only going to last seven years.

The traditional way is to teach you to carry the things that we talk about. You may have them. They're yours. If you want to experiment on yourself, go ahead. You're welcome to it. But one day you might hit the wrong button and end up outside your door and wonder how you got out there. These are also there. I talk about clockwise and counter-clockwise. They both have doorways. But when all the doorways line up at the same time, you have the Bermuda Triangle. That's when you cross over. This is what the spiritual interpreters learn how to do. People think we're really holy. But we just know how to line things up. This is why every spiritual interpreter has the four-leggeds, the wingeds, the water, the sweetgrass and the sage - things to work with. You learn how to line these up.

When you walk this spiritual path, it is yours. You can not appoint yourself God. There are many tests here. These teachings are sacred only to you. Do not try to teach them to others unless you've walked through them and done the grunt work. If you're going to talk about Invision, make sure that you prepare for one year and stay celibate for the last six months. For one year, make sure that you wipe yourself down and put your mind at ease. Be nice to your children. Pray and offer food every morning at 3 a.m. Prepare yourself. Don't jump the gun. It's not like instant coffee and sugar. Do the grunt work of disciplining yourself. These are things we have to do in order to help the people. Anyone can do them.

Chapter 7: The Red Road Today

You know, I've been observing the schools and I've been observing people who are hurting - people who are spiritually bankrupt - and I think we're headed right back to where we were twenty five years ago. Racism is starting to develop again. An altogether different generation is coming out on this Red Road - people who are trying to apply the philosophy of Christian beliefs to this Native way. But in my heart, I strongly feel that it's not going to work. They're confusing their everyday lives with the sincerity of this road. I see people wanting to take things. They want to learn overnight. It hurts me because it took me about forty years to attain the level I'm at today. And it hurts to see these things being desecrated.

People come to my home and demand to know things about my way of life. They come and they say they want power. I tell them, "You are your own power. You have to understand yourself." And they get very angry. It is because the Indian people have always been looked down upon. To this day, society is trained that way. People all over the world do not yet understand the Native way. Yet they want it. But when they find out that there is some grunt work involved - like learning the spiritual laws of the sweat lodge as a firekeeper - they get discouraged and angry.

This is why a lot of us spiritual interpreters get old, hurt and die - because, when we were young, we were strong, so we thought we could handle everything. But we get beaten down. We get tired. When you use up these spiritual interpreters, where else are you going to get somebody to help? Where else are you going to get the teachings? Instead of doing all the listening, pack up and go and learn the grunt work. Learn how to crawl. Learn how to build a fire. Learn how to do all of this so that you gain the valuable experience to pass on to your neighbor. Don't take it home and keep it to yourself. This is what's killing us.

I hope this book will get my point across. I know that it will probably upset a lot of people who want to learn instantly - people who aren't willing to do work at it and do the grunt work of learning how to crawl, then walk, then run. But I hope this book will bring some kind of awareness of the supreme law of North America. We have already gone through the reasons why the four nationalities need to come together. But here in North America, we have the Canunpa - the Sacred Pipe - and laws that go with it.

Nowadays, a lot of young men and women come to me and ask me how they can find themselves. It is a lot harder to do this today than it was in the olden days. It is harder now because we are always exposed to influences, peer pressures and a multicultural way of life. But we must know our roots - who we are, where we come from. In my teachings, I say to my European brothers and sisters, "Before I can help you, please try to understand yourself and find out where your ancestors have come from - your grandmother and your grandfather on both sides. And you will find out that you have a beautiful culture in one of those bloods. You are going to find out that you will be proud of who you are."

I'll tell you a story about a young woman who I trained for eight years. One day she said to me, "Floyd, I'm ready now. I'm OK. I've gotten rid of my early childhood sexual abuse thing. I went to the grandfathers and they said I'm fine. There's nothing wrong with me. After eight years, I'm ready." So I said to her, "All right. If you're ready, why don't you celebrate by having a bad dream?" She got really upset. She said, "You're a medicine man. How can you talk that way? You're supposed to walk with God!" She left and went to my friend's camp. Three months later, I went to the lodge and she was standing there. She gave me tobacco and said, "I'm sorry for what I said. I misunderstood you." I replied, "What are you sorry for? I don't remember what you said. I was speaking the truth. You said you were ready, so I just threw something at you. If you were ready, you would have laughed about it and said, 'OK, I'll do that tonight.'" These are truths that we go through.

Humor is part of my life. I don't scold anyone. I've been taught to speak the truth. If the truth bothers you, it's good, because you're learning and you're remembering where to start. In our teachings, the door swings both ways. If you can't take it, you can leave. And as you go out, don't let it kick you in the butt. But the door swings both ways. When you're ready, you can come back and start again. The spiritual circle in which we live, there's no beginning and there's no end. It's all one circle of equality. The spiritual circle we live by is our grandmother and our mother. She is the image of herself - the moon, the sun and the earth.

I don't like to talk down on anybody. I talk about reality. But if we're going to make a better world here, we have to work together. We have to let go of all our old habits. We are human beings. We are not different from one another. On this island we have a symbol called the Sacred Pipe. That is ours. This is why we have survived for hundreds of years. And the laws of that Sacred Pipe are very simple: walk with humility; walk with respect; help others as you help yourself; give to others as you give to yourself. Listen to what you hear. Do not add on. You're going to hear the things that you are not supposed to do from other people's mouths. Learn with your eyes - you're going to see the things that you're not supposed to do.

What I talk about here is common sense. Today's society does not have common sense. The gift from God is common sense, love and sharing. We the Indian people of North America have never been defeated because we know who we are and we know that we are the roots of this island. We've been here since five B.C. - before Christ, before Columbus, before Custer, before Costner and before casinos - and we'll still be here when they're all gone. The other three nationalities are insecure and uncertain. Their lives are too regulated and they do not recall the grass roots of where they come from. Therefore, they are always in fear of losing something materially. Their respect for each other is not there. They do not shake hands. They do not visit their neighbors. They do not feed each other. And they do not give thanks for whatever they receive day in and day out.

People do not see these things because their mind spirit has been designated intellectually by what I call the "modern-day life curriculum". We have forgotten our roots - who we are and where we come from. This is why we have totally neglected our history. When the "666" took effect in 300 A.D., it began psychological genocide for all mankind. That was when an angel named Lucifer (who, like us, was also the creation of his mother) was given the responsibility to honor the Great Spirit. And he was also given a second command - to honor the weaklings, which is us. Lucifer really got upset about this and he said, "Father, you have asked me to honor you. But why do I have to honor the weaklings as well?" To that, the Great Spirit replied, "Be gone! Go and be well, then come back."

And so Lucifer was cast out by the Great Spirit. But now, he had a power. That power was the mind spirit. Everything that is created by man: a bottle of soda pop, a building, everything man-made, everything you buy - look at it. There's the numbers "666" on it. It's the mark of the beast. That power will only last another five years. During this time, Lucifer is going to use fear to control us. He is using our mind spirit so that we look at each other as different. "You're black, you're yellow, you're white, I'm red, and you have no business coming into the Indian way." I hear that all the time.

One of my elders once said to me, "You prayed for the White Buffalo. The White Buffalo Calf Lady has come. You have seen her vision. Why are you talking to all the nations? You should only talk to the Indian people because that buffalo is ours." But I knew that this was not the message she gave us, so I said to him, "Father, I'm going to speak out of my place, if you allow me. It was Grandpa - your dad - who taught me to go out and join hands with everybody. You have worked for the Bureau of Indian Affairs for thirty years. You didn't want to participate in the ceremonies when I sat with grandpa. And you advise me now to stay away from others. Our white brother gave you a job, a car, a phone, toilet paper - everything you wanted. If you give back everything that he has given you, then I will believe you. Until then, I can not be a hippocrite."

When you teach with the head spirit, your analytical mind is going to teach you evil spirits. You're going to teach bad medicine. In all the years I have been walking since 1948, the only bad medicine I have run into is marijuana and alcohol - and psychology. If somebody calls you at 3 a.m. and says, "I'm going to kick your door in at 3:30, and I'm going to beat you up at 3:35," you're going to get up and barricade the doors and windows. You're going to sit there with a baseball bat in your hands, watching the time. That's psychology. The Great Spirit did not create evil spirits. An angel created them - an angel who was confused. His name was Lucifer. He is still a creation of God. But the head spirit is what he uses to control us.

This analytical way of life that we have adopted is killing us. We don't listen. We are supposed to learn with our eyes, listen with our hearts and speak the truth with our tongues. But all we do today is sit in front of the TV. Our younger generation is at risk. The Lady said that on the 21st day of the 21st year of the 21st century there will be an alignment and that the four horsemen will return. We must help our children live beyond the next twenty-six years. It makes me sad that our children are lost now. It's not their fault. We as parents need to take our children in our hands and love them. This way they won't grow up and get involved in gangs. They won't be looking for T.L.C. from other sources. They'll teach people not to destroy something that is not ours because we are only here to use these things temporarily. We're not going to live a thousand years. Teach one another love. Help one another. Learn to shake hands. That's all I ask. Don't be self-centered. Don't be selfish. Don't think you're better than your neighbor. Don't ignore the person on the street. Buy him a coffee. Get him some food. Because you never know, he could be the Great Spirit in disguise testing you.

Do not be mean to your children. When I raise my voice to my children, I know it's to discipline them, but it hurts me. Sometimes I sit down and cry because in a different time when I was brought up - in the 1940's and 50's - it was a different world. We can only dream about those days. They're gone now. Nowadays, we practically have to lead our children by the hand. We constantly have to remind them every moment what they're supposed to do. Only love and T.L.C. and listening to our children will teach them discipline and how to do things for themselves. Take your children on a trip. Show them where the sacred places are. This life is very short and we're running out of time.

This journey that we are taking together involves all of us - not just one nationality. Over five hundred years ago, when the Lady came back, she said, "I have brought you the sacred gift of survival - to walk quietly, to help others as you help yourself, to love people as you would love yourself, to respect others as you respect yourself, to set an example for your children, to hold out your hand, to love and bring everybody together, and to say thank you for your life." These are the energies that she gave us to carry. The spiritual circle of the universe is 360 degrees - a holistic circle. Here in North America, we worship the White Buffalo Calf Lady, Guadeloupe, the Blessed Virgin Mary, Corn Lady. We do not separate these images. We do not separate spirit.

When I say the power of the woman has returned, I get a lot of threats from militia groups and such. They think that when you pray for the nation and the White Buffalo, it means that all the Indian people are coming back to reorganize the American Indian Movement. Back in 1994, we had ceremonies over here for our brothers at Oka when they had their problems, because they wouldn't let us go over there. The FBI, the CIA - they had our names right at the borders. But our hearts went out to our brothers. Never give up what you're doing. Do it for your children. Do it for your spiritual fathers and your uncles. Do it for them. Let this drum be heard all over the nation. All you ladies, sisters - support your children, support your man. Your power is coming.

The nations of the world are all coming back. Like Grandpa Frank said, "One day, they are going to hear the voice of that drum once again. And one day, that Canunpa, the Sacred Pipe, is going to journey back and unite all the nations together." Every nation in this world will come back one day. The Hunting Chief will make sure that everyone has enough to eat. The Camp Chief will make sure that everybody has a place to sit down. The Medicine Chief - an Indian psychologist - will talk to the people. The War Chief will be the protector of the nation. And then the Speaking Chief, the M.C., whatever you want to call him. And then there is the Decision Chief - that is what I am. I don't make decisions. I just hear the chiefs talk. I sit there and listen to the stories and, when I think about it I stand up and say, "This is the way it's going to be." And everybody says, "Aho". Nobody can say anything about it because they know it's the right decision.

It doesn't matter what nationality we are, we all come from our mother. We are one blood. I don't care if you're black, red, yellow, white, green - whatever. The blood we spill is the same. We are relatives. In our journey, on our destiny, there are no mistakes and no failures. It is up to us to get up and walk. Never say anything bad to anyone and you will get along very well. If you see an elder sitting, get him a drink because some day you're going to be there. I go to hospitals. I look for elders. I sit with them and I pray with them until they journey home. I go to old age homes. How many of you go visit them at Christmas? How many of you get baskets together - round up food from your friends at Christmas time - and go give it to the elders? Do your share of work while you are here on this earth because you are only here a short time.

Our brothers of the other three sacred colors - our white brother, our yellow brother and our black brother - are looking forward to joining us on this journey. And so I ask you, my Indian brothers and sisters, to teach them wisely. Teach them not to desecrate. Teach them with respect because our blood is one. Do not desecrate yourself by judging people of other nationalities and telling them that they have no right to be on your path. Some of my brothers have this problem because they have been hurt for many years. But it is all right to be hurt because the hurt that you have experienced is a success in your life.

We haven't lost anything. We have not forgotten. It is still there beside the road. We don't need to think negatively of each other. We don't need to be superstitious. The only bad medicine that will ever come your way is your head. It can make you gear yourself up and stay up all night. Black, red, yellow and white - we have not lost this holistic way that we all live. It's just been set aside temporarily. Now, pick it up. But if you're going to pick up this spiritual holistic way of life, learn how to give. If you want help and teach, you need to get up. You have a job. You have money. You have a car. Go to the elder and bring him food. Do not desecrate him!

In that sacred belief, you walk quietly with sensitivity. You help others as you are helped. You have compassion and love. If you see an elder standing, give him a chair. Walk with a good attitude and set a good example. Give thanks for this life. If you want to walk this red road, you get up every morning at 3 a.m. and pray. Be ready to hold out your hand and help the child, the mother, the grandmother. Be there for them. These are small things but this brings back our children. Do not leave your children at home. They are the ones who are going to bring us back together. Do not leave your children at home when the elders are talking. When we ask our elders to do something, bring them tobacco - a gift. Do not give them a sacred cigarette. You have elders in the community. Feed them. Have their food put together. Honor your children, honor each one. Feed them, for we are one.

Make life your humor. Tell jokes to yourself. Look in the mirror and tell yourself how beautiful you are. It's hard for us to do that because we're afraid to look ourselves in the eye. Yet we can look at everybody around us. That's because we're shame-based. It's caused by somebody keeping us down - "don't do this, don't do that." European culture teaches that - "don't touch this, don't touch that, go to bed at 9 o'clock..." Leave the children alone. If they learn by hard knocks, then they're going to be better people. You stunt their learning of reality - touching hands-on - by constantly trying to control them. If you're very materialistic, then you have no right to bring up children. Material stuff is material stuff. You can always replace it. But you can never replace that child - that wonderful gift from God.

How many of you know love? How many of you sat with your fathers and grandfathers and listened to their stories? When you fell down, did they pick you up, wipe your hands and tell you everything was OK? How many of you are respected with love, where you have birthdays and they make a meal for you and feed the spirits. It is in the giving that we shall receive, they say. The family makes a feast so that everybody will be proud. How many of you got love and hope from your grandfather, your father, your brother, or your companion? Did they listen to you or were they always hollering at you, telling you what to do? How many of you have been through that? It hurts. We come here with nothing and we go with nothing. The only part of life that we have in common is death. Until then, these teachings of love, called "tender loving care," is what the nation that will survive will have once again.

Now, I'm going to ask you to say five good things about yourself. Go ahead. The society we grew up in taught us to always be ashamed of ourselves. You can give out a lot of love but you can get yourself into trouble giving out too much. Learn how to give to yourself. Look at yourself and tell yourself how beautiful you are. Say, "I've got a beautiful nose, I've got beautiful eyes, I've got a beautiful smile, I'm handsome, I'm pretty." I call that "self-T.L.C." Look in the mirror every morning and say that to get yourself going. It works. Teach yourself that and you won't have any tension or ulcers.

Learn how to love yourself because you can't give any love out unless you love yourself. That's why I teach the healing of hate. We have to heal the hate within our nation, within our community and within our home. The beauty is within us. Tell yourself that every morning. Pretty soon, you will believe it. When you walk in a crowd, you are representing the many generations of your family. You are your ancestors. You are the four-legged, the winged. The code of ethics you set for yourself - the example you set in public - is what you have to be at home. Forty-five minutes belongs to each and every one of us to prepare to go out in public. If you're always late for work, move back that forty-five minutes.

Many of my brothers are looking for themselves today. They travel everywhere, always looking. I went through that period myself. I went looking. Finally, I returned home and my grandfather looked at me and said, "Did you find it?" I never answered him. It's inside of you. All you need to do is give yourself some time and look, and you will see yourself. Go into the Sweat Lodge and you will find yourself. You're in there. But remember, don't get too "wakan" - too holy. Remember that example. Remember that we are each other's teachers.

Look good and feel good because the learning on the Red Road, which is our blood, is the attitude and example that we get from our elders plus the society we live in. You are dynamite. You are only you. The Sacred Pipe does not teach you to carry other people around you. It doesn't teach you to run somebody's life or that they have to be like you. The Sacred Pipe teaches you the extended family, compassion, the beginning, the angel that is that little child - innocent, beautiful, pure. Are you so sensitive that you get angry quickly? Are you happy, laughing all the time? That is the combination of balance in this world. Learn how to use both of them. When somebody teaches by saying something about you, don't say anything. I teach people to never speak for me and never stick up for me. This journey is mine. If someone doesn't like the way I walk and talk on this journey, let them stay home.

Each one of us learns our own road. And each one of us travels down that road at our own speed. No matter how we do it, we're all going to get there at the same time. Some day, we're all going to go home. One day, you will look back down the Red Road and say, "Grandfathers, I thank you for letting me serve you." And at the end of your time, the Great Spirit will help you. Our spirit will always live on. The only respect and dignity we all have in common is in death. Until then, walk with respect. And as you walk, remember - the road to success is always under construction on this Red Road.

So let us all put our minds together and have Tunkasila, the Great Spirit, bless us. At this moment, let us listen with our hearts, not with our head spirit. And also, during this time, I would like to ask each and every one to listen to each other - carefully.

Oh, Tunkasila, Gitchi Manitou, Heavenly Father, we gather here to hear the message that the spirit Lady has given us. You have given us the time, at the turn of the century, where everything will change for the better. But, for the time being, help all of us who initiate this concern for Mother Earth and our generations to come to put our minds together, join hands and say "thank you" for allowing us to be here together as a family.

Aho! Mitakuye Oyasin.

Index